GAME PLAN

PRACTICAL WISDOM FOR THE COLLEGE EXPERIENCE

nic gibson and syler thomas

foreword by scot mcknight

author of *The Jesus Creed for Students*

PARACLETE PRESS
BREWSTER, MASSACHUSETTS

To all the students to whom we have ministered:
sharing our lives with you has made us the pastors we are today.

And to our own children: Abigail, Rachel Claire, and Jude Gibson;
and Kaila, Ellie, Foster, and Grace Thomas. Our greatest desire is that you might know
the God of all knowledge and wisdom.

Game Plan: Practical Wisdom for the College Experience

2016 Third Printing
2015 Second Printing
2012 First Printing

Copyright © 2012 by Nicola Gibson and Syler Thomas

ISBN 978-1-61261-111-2

Unless otherwise noted, all Scripture references are taken from the Holy Bible, New International Version®, NIV®, Copyright © 1973, 1978, 1984 by Biblica, Inc.™ Used by permission of Zondervan. All rights reserved worldwide.

Scripture references labeled NASB are taken from the NEW AMERICAN STANDARD BIBLE®, Copyright © 1960, 1968, 1971, 1972, 1973, 1975, 1977, 1995 by The Lockman Foundation. Used by permission.

Library of Congress Cataloging-in-Publication Data
Gibson, Nic.
  Game plan : practical wisdom for the college experience / Nic Gibson and Syler Thomas ; foreword by Scot McKnight.
     p. cm.
  ISBN 978-1-61261-111-2 (trade pbk.)
  1. College students—Religious life. 2. Universities and colleges—Religion. I. Thomas, Syler. II. Title.
  BV4531.3.G53 2012
  248.8'34—dc23   2012000362

10 9 8 7 6 5 4 3

Published by Paraclete Press
Brewster, Massachusetts
www.paracletepress.com
Printed in the United States of America.

CONTENTS

Odd chapters written by Nic Gibson | **Even chapters written by Syler Thomas**

FOREWORD

Recently I was staring into the faces of about ten high school students, each contemplating life in college, when a young pastor asked me this: What would you tell these students about how to keep their faith when they go off to college? Having taught college students for nearly two decades, and having seen some of them make a wreck of their faith as a result of bad choices, the question probed one of the deepest questions I ponder as a professor. *How does a young man or young woman sustain faith in the turbulence of transition from home to college and beyond?*

There are, of course, no easy answers. What that transition reveals is that faith is often sustained, however unknown to the ones who have faith, by a family, by a group of friends, and by a schedule that permits less freedom and more predictable (and controlled) behaviors. But when the college student wakes up on Day One in college at least these elements of life have been radically changed: mom and dad are not there to guide, friends are mostly (or totally) in other schools, a schedule is now completely free—which means one can stay up and out all night long, one can choose to sleep in and one can choose with whom one sleeps and what one eats and drinks, and how much of any of the aforementioned items. That's when faith matters even more. Why? Because now faith is solely, or at least much more, the choice of the fresh college student. And that choice is not easy. Church was often connected to friends, and without friends at the church it's harder to go and harder to participate; and getting up is harder because a routine schedule, mostly shaped by mom and dad, is interrupted.

You are on your own, and what you do is your choice. Choose wisely.

That is why this book by Nic Gibson and Syler Thomas is so important. I would advise you to take *Game Plan: Practical Wisdom for the College Experience* with you to college. I would recommend you find a quiet place for the first two or three weeks to read one chapter in a setting, and ask yourself these basic questions: Is this true of me? Are these the situations I'm facing? How am I doing? What does my faith mean to me today? Nic and Syler have touched on the real topics and real questions that will invade your life the minute you set foot on campus. Now I'd like to raise that recommendation one notch: find a wise friend with whom you can read and discuss the topics of *Game Plan*. Live this book together for a month.

What you do in that first month or two may well have a big impact on what kind of college experience you have and, not to be too dramatic, what happens in the rest of your life. What happens in college doesn't stay in college; it shapes where you go and what you become.

Scot McKnight
North Park University

 **INTRODUCTION**

We the authors first met each other on a bright and brisk autumn Saturday morning at a church-league flag football game in front of a local middle school. Our friendship grew as we began ministering to high school students together, but also as we continued to play football, softball, and (our favorite) pick-up basketball. We also both tended to exhibit a great deal of competitiveness in our different athletic endeavors. Even though we knew that winning or losing whatever game we were playing didn't matter in the grand scheme of things, we both felt passionately that playing a game to win is what makes it worth playing. And in order to win a game, you have to have a game plan.

Similarly, being successful at college doesn't happen by accident. Having a well thought-out game plan is crucial to a college experience filled with joy and not regret. It is no secret that college carries incredible opportunities for growth, along with significant potential for your faith to suffer. The key to all that follows, which also happens to be one of the great themes in the Bible, is wisdom. It is not without some honesty that universities label first-year students "fresh" and second-year students "sophomore," a term meaning a foolish person under the delusion that he is wise.

This book was then written out of this conviction and out of our other intense passion. Our conviction is that the college experience requires wisdom. Our passion is to see our own students, and the students of other schools and churches, thrive in faith and grow in wisdom in college: to see you emerge from college with your faith not only intact, but at the center of your life. Our hope is that the Game Plan that follows will be a part of helping this to happen.

We've also asked some friends of ours to share their own stories after every other chapter. Our hope is that their stories will provide some real-life experiences to reinforce what we share.

Thank you to all the students who have helped us write this book. Those who have put its teaching into practice have given us even greater comfort. Besides our families, you are the great work of our lives, and our boast in the day Christ returns.

Special thanks to Paul Soupiset and Wendy Woodnick, who were invaluable in publishing earlier versions of this material.

Thanks also to the many nonstudent editors who read these chapters and offered their input, especially our wives, Alexi and Heidi.

Finally, you may disagree with some of our conclusions. Feel free. Use this book as a springboard for a discussion with your friends. The exchange of ideas, and not just the downloading of them, is where you learn the most. In fact, we have tried our best to keep the chapters short so that you will do more thinking for yourself, not less.

To God be the glory, now and forever.

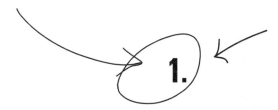

1.

SURVIVING
A SECULAR SCHOOL

I remember sitting with my good friend and kayaking mentor, Guy Rocker, and looking down forty-five feet into what is called Rocket Ride Rapid on New York's Black River. As is common in white water kayaking, we had pulled out above the rapid and were scouting out the dangers of this obstacle, carefully choosing a course of action. For the veteran paddlers this was a cakewalk, but for a beginner like me this was a deceivingly hazardous rapid because of three converging dangers.

The first was a twenty-five-foot drop that, though it looked fun, could also easily leave you bottom side up. Then after the drop, the river doglegs left, creating a huge eddy on the right, making the river flow hard against a huge rock wall and then jut off to the left. Last, Guy said that under that rock wall, just below the surface of the water, was a large chamber that had been carved out over time by the river.

Over the years certain rafters and paddlers had gotten trapped in it when the river was high, and only some had made it out. Guy warned me as we went to our boats, "I know you've done harder rapids, but take this one very seriously. If you do what I told you, you'll be fine."

Things went fine on that and all the other rapids that day, and by 3:00 p.m., I had paddled the hardest river I have ever done. More than that, though, I had learned valuable lessons about the water and, specifically, I had learned how multiplying dangers can make rapids look exciting, but can also make them deadly.

This is the best way I can try to prepare you for the college ride. Many students reading this book will be going to secular colleges. By "secular" I mean an institution that is either totally indifferent to and often antagonistic to the gospel of Jesus Christ, or a school that has sufficiently drifted from Christian roots so that what remains of those roots is often more harmful than good.

In secular schools there is a convergence of three dangers to faith that we need to take a minute to scout out from "above," and then carefully plan a course of action intended to avoid the dangers, yet still enjoy the ride and conquer the rapid. As you are making your way through college, you have the opportunity not only to survive, but also thrive if you have a spiritual plan of action (a Game Plan, if you will) and if you execute that plan with some discipline. Let me also point out that these dangers are present to some degree in Christian colleges as well, so even those headed to a Christian school would do well to read on.

Three converging dangers

The transition between high school and college is a tremendous change for most students in at least three ways:

First, you now have almost unlimited freedom. There are no curfews. There are no homework police. There are no bed times, or even recommended bed times. You can do whatever you want, whenever you want, and there is no accountability about anything short of National Guard intervention. This freedom can make you a well-disciplined and fun adult, but it can also shipwreck your faith and ruin your college experience.

Second, added to this freedom is the reality that you are leaving the Christian community you have been a part of in high school. Hopefully, in high school you were close enough with some other believers, your parents, and your youth pastor that they could get in your face about God and help you grow. In college it is common for you to walk into your dorm room, watch your parents leave, and come to the realization that no human you know back home is going to know what happens here unless you tell them. There is no accountability. Zero. This complete freedom with no accountability is an opportunity as well as a danger.

The third danger is the assault on the mind and heart that comes from anti-Christian ideologies. Concerning the mind, wading through the intellectual nonsense of many modern philosophies in every contemporary department can be incredibly confusing for anyone, but is all the more difficult for intellectual beginners.[1] It is an insufferable maze of muddled logic made more depressing by the countless casualties of faith publicized by certain antagonistic professors or students. And don't be fooled that this is only the case if you major in philosophy, and will not assail you in, say, the English department, or even chemistry or business. The prevailing secular philosophies of relativism and pluralism permeate all departments—especially departments of literature, business, and religion.

Your Christian worldview will be either openly confronted or blatantly ignored as irrelevant in almost every course. It is common, if you open your mouth to defend your view, to be treated as a naïve backcountry redneck, one of the last remaining fossils of a bygone age of "ignorant fundamentalist enthusiasm." To the person unaware of this coming trial, it can be overwhelming—even to the death of faith.

---

1. It should go without saying, but it is important to understand that an "intellectual beginner" is what you are in your undergraduate studies. For some this will be hard to accept, but it is a very important point to concede. Accepting that you are an intellectual novice will help you interact with your professors more humbly. It will also keep you from believing that if you cannot solve a theological or biblical difficulty, you need to throw away your faith to be intellectually honest. To do so is merely pride, since most undergraduates do not have the academic skills yet to work through many intellectual difficulties related to Christian faith. Being humble concerning these problems will get you communicating with a trusted spiritual mentor.

Parallel to this assault on the Christian mind is an equally strong assault on your heart. This assault is the hedonism of college culture. Hedonism is the belief that your own personal self-gratification is the highest good. 1 Peter 4:1–5 says:

Therefore, since Christ suffered in his body, arm yourselves also with the same attitude, because he who has suffered in his body is done with sin. As a result, he does not live the rest of his earthly life for evil human desires, but rather for the will of God. For you have spent enough time in the past doing what pagans choose to do—living in debauchery, lust, drunkenness, orgies, carousing and detestable idolatry. They think it strange that you do not plunge with them into the same flood of dissipation, and they heap abuse on you. But they will have to give account to him who is ready to judge the living and the dead.

I remember thinking it strange in my early years as a Christian that Paul, as well as Peter, would talk so much about drunkenness and sexual promiscuity of many kinds, including orgies. Then I went to college. During my first semester I put this Scripture above my desk as a constant reminder. Pornography is everywhere, from your roommate's trunk, to the community bathroom stalls, to movies playing in the lounge right outside your door. At many schools there are simply no sexual boundaries. None. You'll see what I mean. Students often drown themselves in a fountain of various pleasures available at every turn. You will have to face this temptation of hedonism, too.

Although any one of these dangers may be manageable to the sincere Christ follower, added together they can wear down even the brightest mind and most passionate heart.

The multiplied danger to biblical faith

Picture it. You arrive at your dorm or apartment, unpack your things, and watch your sweet but blubbering parents begin to make the trip home. In the next two weeks, people clearly more intellectually accomplished than your high school teachers and youth pastor make the following arguments:

1. You are certainly not the creative, loving art of a personal, purposeful God, but the impersonal result of matter plus chance plus time in a random, pitiless universe.
2. The Bible is religiously untrustworthy, and to think it can be "simply" or "literally" interpreted is quite naïve. The Bible, like all great religious texts, is only the religious expression of ancient people, is hardly relevant, and is certainly not authoritative.
3. There is no single true "Truth," only perception and experience. To say there is any truth or absolute morality is arrogant and intolerant (insert a very morally disappointed facial expression here), and to say that your "experience" with Jesus is somehow "The" religious experience is unthinkably small-minded.

How does one respond to this? Paul, the painfully realistic apostle, said it best. He conceded that if the above was true then, "Let us eat and drink, for tomorrow we die."

The meaningless world of many contemporary philosophies spirals us into a world where all that is left is sensation and belonging. All we have left is the escape to pleasurable sensations that can easily be found in alcohol, illicit substances, and casual sexual recreation.

So you have the institutional promotion of this meaningless worldview, and you are invited by your peers to look for meaning in diversions, intimacy, and belonging. Now add to that a complete lack of any accountability. Your pastor isn't there to help you with these intellectual struggles. You have no one with a common commitment to follow Jesus through the intellectual wasteland, and you don't even have to leave your dorm's floor to partake in sensual opportunities. Before you know it, social freedom has become spiritual loneliness, and very few have a heart and mind strong enough to weather this storm alone. Do you see the problem?

Charting a course

So we've taken a tiny glance at three converging dangers to faith in Christ at a secular school. I hope you can feel the obstacles that will be presented to your faith in such a way that you are motivated to prepare for them. This can be a dangerous time, and your life in God hangs in the balance. This is a season of your life that you should anticipate with great excitement, but also with serious thought regarding its successful navigation, especially as it relates to God. Lose Him and you have lost all. In light of this, I offer the following three courses of action.

First is the establishment of regular and meaningful times of Bible reading and prayer ("quiet times"). There is no substitute for this universal Christian need, and as a pastor I can say it is one of the two clearest determining factors to long-term growth and health in a person's faith. Yet I have heard countless people tell me, "I just can't read the Bible." You must overcome obstacles and excuses with creativity and discipline. Do you have AD/HD? So do I. Are you dyslexic? Get the Bible in digital audio files. Do you have poor reading comprehension? Get an easy-to-read translation like the New Living Bible or The Message.

There's an old worship song called "In the Secret" with this line: "Pressing onward, pushing every hindrance aside, out of my way; 'Cause I want to know you more!" Discipline yourself in the area of Bible reading joyfully, not as a duty, but as spiritual training, and you will likely thrive. Neglect this call and no matter how much dutiful guilt you feel, you will not fully succeed as a disciple of Jesus. I cannot claim that I am a devout "learner" of a teacher unless I make learning his teaching a consistent priority. Nor can you.

Second, engage in deliberate and regular Christian fellowship (Syler writes on this in chapter 8, but it is worth hitting on twice). This may be in the context of a campus fellowship, a church large group meeting, a Bible study, regular worship, or a living situation. The context of fellowship is not as important as its existence. Hebrews 10:25 says, "Let us not give up meeting together, as some are in the habit of doing, but let us encourage one another—and all the more as you see the Day approaching." Scripture makes plain that following Christ is a team affair.

Although, as discussed above, we each do individual training as disciples, we are meant to live out the faith together through what is called "community" or "fellowship." In fact, Scripture teaches that we are to participate in both personal and corporate Bible study, worship, and prayer. The things we do alone we are also to do together.

By "fellowship" (now often called "community") I do not mean hanging out with Christians, although that is fun and good. Fellowship is the means by which we share our lives with each other on consistently deepening levels. Deep relating among Christians cannot long ignore spiritual things and the encouragement of spiritual growth among those in the community of Christ. Through meaningful Christian fellowship we find God's intention for how his community is to work. We find people who will look deeply at Scripture and its implications with us; confront sin in us for our own good; care for us when we are in need; accept our care when they are in need; and experience the working of the Holy Spirit together with us. By experiencing life together we all become healthier, deeper, and stronger disciples of Jesus. Remember Ecclesiastes 4:12, "Though one may be overpowered, two can defend themselves. A cord of three strands is not quickly broken."

Third, find a spiritual mentor. For many, your colleges will have paid staff workers whose calling is to help you grow in your faith. Others will not. If your campus does have such people, I would start with them. Others will find college staff and faculty members who are believers, graduate students, or people in your church who are farther along in the faith than you are.

There are three criteria that are essential for a possible mentor. First, you should sense a deep authenticity in his or her love and devotion to Christ, the church, and the Bible. Second, you should sense that she or he is an experienced, seasoned, and clear thinker who has already dealt with many of the issues you will be facing. Third, find someone who is a match with your intellectual temperament, but not your sins. There is some similarity needed, but you do not want someone so like you that they cannot help you because of your shared spiritual blind spots. If you are passive, find someone who will challenge you. If you tend to exhaust your emotions with your thinking, find someone who thinks deeply, but doesn't get all worked up over figuring every little thing out.

Remember also, good mentors are usually well-disciplined people who live full lives. If you take their time, give back so that you will not be a burden on them. Find some way to save them time as they invest time in you. Babysit their kids or do the dishes if you visit for a meal. However, the best way to repay them is always by living wholeheartedly for Christ for the rest of your life. Nothing brings a mentor—or a youth pastor—more joy.

2.

DEALING WITH
THE DATING SCENE

My first hint that college was going to be different from high school came during my first weekend at DePaul University. I don't know if it's that Chicago girls are more forward than the polite Texas girls I was used to, but I was not exactly ready for them to be invading my personal space uninvited. On a "Welcome to Chicago" tour of the city that included a boat ride on Lake Michigan, a girl I had just met was putting her hands on my legs during our conversation as though we were married. "I can barely remember your name," I thought, "and now you're touching my leg?"

A couple months later, at a Halloween party, things got even more interesting. Picture this. For my Halloween costume, I dress up as packaging material. Basically, I wrap myself in bubble wrap, fashion a pointy hat out of the same material, make a big "Silica Gel—Do Not Eat" sign and tape it to my bubbles. So here I am, sitting on a couch at a party with lots of upperclassmen, lots of drinking, lots of smoking, and I'm there as Bubble Wrap. "What's your name?" I hear. It's the voice of a fourth-year redhead, sitting next to me. I recognize her as one of the stars of the most recent play in the Theatre School. "Hello," I respond, adjusting my bubbles.

A conversation ensues, the topic of which I can't recall, mostly because, following the pattern of the boat ride girl before her, she invades my personal space like a marauding bandit, and begins grabbing my hand and pulling it down between her leg and mine. "I'll send her a hint that I'm not interested," I think. So I sort of smile and chuckle, pull my hand away, and keep talking. We talk some more, but then she grabs my hand again, and pulls it down. I pull my hand away again. She isn't getting the hint.

Finally, apparently bored with our patty cake, she goes for it. Leaning over, she whispers in my ear: "Walk me home," gets up, and walks away. I'm left on the couch, thinking: "Lady! Why are you doing this to me? There are any number of other young men in this room who would love to hold your hand, walk you home, and perhaps stay awhile. You're messing with the wrong dude. Come on, I'm the flippin' bubble-wrap boy!" Thankfully, I never saw her again. But I thought: we're not in Kansas anymore, Toto. Not to say that those of you heading to Kansas won't experience the same struggles. You get the idea.

I realize this story is relatively tame compared to many that could be told. I share it simply to illustrate that even though you might have faced some serious temptations relating to the opposite sex in high school, it certainly doesn't let up. In fact, in most cases, it gets a lot more challenging and complicated. So my advice on how to respond to these situations is to wear bubble wrap everywhere you go. OK, not really.

Of course, what would college be without the opposite sex? Imagine all of the work that could actually be accomplished if our schools weren't co-ed! Although I'm not so sure, given the presence of the Internet, video games, and ESPN. So maybe it's just the women who would get some work done. Regardless, you must have a Game Plan on how you will interact with the opposite sex.

A good thing

First, I want to make perfectly clear that men and women relating with one another is a very normal, important, and healthy thing, something that God is in favor of. One of the reasons why the Shakers (a denomination of Christians in the 1700s) didn't gain widespread popularity in their day was that they believed it was wrong for men and women to interact. (This also meant that there were no Shaker babies, if you know what I mean. So much for church growth the old-fashioned way.) God has made men and women to live and work and play together, and this is a great thing. The complicated part is that God has not only made us intellectual and emotional beings; he's also made us sexual beings. When men and women gather together, there is a level of interaction that cannot be ignored, and that is the sexual dynamic.

I'll never forget the realization I came to when I was a freshman in college. I was what one would call a "flagrant flirter," but was person-ally unaware of it. I was talking to a friend of mine about a high school girl I had befriended on an out-of-town retreat, explaining that we had been writing a lot, that she had told me many of her problems, and that I was really trying to help her. He very politely but firmly made it clear that this was a situation where she could easily get emotion-ally attached to me, and that if he were in my situation, he certainly wouldn't want that to happen. I remember leaving that conversation feeling offended. What right does he have to tell me what to do? He doesn't know the whole situation! The nerve!

But as I began to reflect on my interactions with girls, I realized that I had a glaringly obvious pattern of befriending cute girls. I looked at my prayer list, and as I remember it, at least 80 percent of the people on the list were girls. I really thought my heart was pure! I had ulterior motives, namely that I wanted these girls to like me in the same way that I liked them.

The Hazy

It was about the same time that my best friend, Britt, was coming to the same realization. We were relatively popular guys, both in our youth group and with people from churches around our state with whom we did statewide retreats. Britt and I both had to admit that there were girls literally all over the state with whom we had developed what we called a "hazy relationship" or "hazy" for short. A hazy is a friendship where both parties are clearly attracted, there's a whole lot of flirting going on, but neither party talks about it. In our case, we didn't consider ourselves "players" at all; we thought our motives were pretty clean. We weren't acting on these attractions to feed our physical desires. But without a doubt, we were feeding an emotional hunger for girls to notice us.

To give you an example of just how mixed up all of my motives and desires were, when I first showed up at college, I met a girl on my floor who was a Christian and shared some of my passion for God. Excited about the opportunity to connect with someone who was a fellow believer, and so that we could encourage each other in our faith, I suggested that we pray together in the basement of the building. So every now and again we'd go downstairs into an empty study room, we'd (get this) hold hands, and pray. And you can just take a wild guess as to whether she was cute or not. Bingo. I'm embarrassed to share this story, but I really was clueless at the time. Let me take this opportunity to state what should be obvious at this point. Guys and girls should not be prayer partners, nor should they be accountability partners. Furthermore, it is almost impossible for one to have a deep, completely platonic relationship with the opposite sex. Romance will always enter the picture one way or another, which is fine as long as the person is a good match for you. Long-term romantic relationships often form when a guy and girl who are not initially attracted to each other become best friends, and grow to love each other. This is great. But if you are interested in someone, just be honest about it and pursue the relationship. Or don't. Avoid the hazy middle ground.

The way out: Guarding your heart

A much-quoted Proverb on this subject is 4:23: "Guard your heart, for it is the wellspring of life." If you've heard this quoted so many times that it has lost its meaning, I encourage you to take a deeper look. The first half is an entreaty to guard our hearts. Pick whatever mental image you like: a security guard at a bank, a Secret Service agent guarding the president, an offensive lineman guarding his quarterback. These people's job is to guard: no one will steal the treasure in these vaults, no one will harm the commander-in-chief, no one will sack my quarterback. We guard something because it's valuable. Why is your heart worth guarding?

The second clause gives us the reason why: because the heart is what nourishes our life. The New Living Translation interprets this clause as: "for it affects everything you do." The importance of maintaining the health of our heart, that is, the well-being of our emotional state, cannot be overstated. God gave us a very wonderful and dangerous thing when he gave us our emotions. They can make us feel wonderful, and they can also steer the ship of our life far off course. The stirring of our hearts can lead us to attempt wonderful and noble things, and it also can lead us toward great folly. When men and women interact, there is potential for our guards to come down, and for our hearts to be opened up. And if they get broken, it really will affect everything we do.

For some reason, when it comes to romantic relationships, we tend to do the exact opposite of guarding our hearts. We put our hearts on display. We offer them around like they're food samples at the supermarket. Anybody interested in trying some of this heart? How about you? Anyone at all care to take it? In fact, when some of us hear this advice to guard our hearts, we think: come on, you're just trying to take my fun away. Wrong. The advice to guard our hearts is actually intended to create more fun. That is, unless your idea of fun is weeping in your roommate's arms because you got your heart broken. Anyone who has had his or her heart broken can tell you that the advice is there to protect you from the pain of an unguarded heart.

The "unequal yoke"

This is especially important when we consider dating someone who doesn't share our core beliefs. Many of you have heard a verse from 2 Corinthians quoted and have gotten the message that you're "not supposed to date non-Christians," but perhaps you don't know why. Let me try to spell it out for you. The verse in question is 2 Corinthians 6:14, which begins: "Do not be yoked together with unbelievers." Paul is not talking specifically about romantic relationships here, but is laying down the general principle that believers should avoid forming close relationships with nonbelievers *that would cause them to potentially compromise their beliefs.* The yoke metaphor relates to farming, where two animals are joined together by a wooden beam called a yoke.

So what's the big deal if I just go on a date with a non-Christian? I don't intend to be connected to anyone by a wooden beam! The reality is that it is OK for you to go on a date with a non-Christian, if you define dating as a man and a woman hanging out together, staying at a surface level emotionally. The problem is that our culture has moved toward the definition of dating as two people consumed with one another. Not to mention the fact that for a Christian, dating should be about discovering who your future spouse will be. And while there are some stories out there of dating relationships where one of the two isn't a Christian and gets converted later on, these are the exception.

When you decide to date a non-Christian, even casually, you are opening yourself up to the possibility that you could fall in love with this person, at which point you are faced with the prospect of either breaking it off (and breaking two hearts) or yoking yourself with a person who doesn't share your life priorities. Trust me when I tell you that you must be vigilant about guarding your heart around attractive non-Christians with whom you connect emotionally. Of the Christians I knew whose faith faltered in college, dating non-Christians was easily the leading contributor.

Some of you who have never struggled with this might be thinking: this won't be a problem for me! I won't fall for someone who isn't a Christian! I'll know better than that. There are two problems here.

First, our hearts don't care what their religious beliefs are. Our hearts say: "That's for the head to work through. From my standpoint, this is the most incredible human being I've ever met, and I'm going for it." Once the heart is hooked, it's close to impossible to move on. And you find yourself in love with someone who isn't the best possible match for you. So there must be a combination of the heart and the head working together. It's the head's job to allow the heart to become interested when the head determines it's a good choice, and for its own good, the heart needs to obey. I'm reminded of the song "Hopelessly Devoted to You" from Grease. Sandy sings: "My head is saying, 'Fool, forget him.' My heart is saying, 'Don't let go.'" So which does she listen to? Her heart, of course. And they live happily ever after (more about this in a later chapter).

Don't trust your heart when your head is trying to make the decision for you. Why? Because your head functions as the guardian for your heart. It is the primary safeguard for the treasure that is your heart. Trust it, or you are bound to make some pretty poor choices when it comes to whom you pursue romantically.

The second problem is that it is extremely difficult to make the choice between a God who is not physically present with you and someone who is not only physically present, but physically attractive, intellectually stimulating, and who makes you laugh. When those two are weighed against each other, the delayed gratification of enjoying and honoring God will be hard to compete with the immediate satisfaction of dating a dynamite person who is a long-term bad choice. But don't wander from the Game Plan. Remember what your goal is: honoring God, not feeding your flesh.

Having said all that, I also want to point out that just because someone can check the "Christian" box doesn't necessarily mean that dating them is a great idea. Nor does it mean that you don't have to guard your heart. Ideally, you want to look for someone whose satisfaction in life comes from knowing Jesus, not you. If you start there, you're headed in the right direction.

Boundaries

Another way of looking at the concept of guarding your heart is to think about it in terms of setting up boundaries. For many, the idea of having boundaries in relationships feels frustrating and unnecessary. "Why do we have to worry about all that junk? Let's just have fun!" The reality is that boundaries enable you to enjoy the gifts God has for you all the more.

Some boundaries might include things like deciding that you're not going to be alone with a member of the opposite sex past midnight. Our guards are definitely down when we're tired, so avoiding late-night situations is key. Or you may find it helpful to have a close, same-sex friend with whom you can share your thoughts, desires, and struggles. Knowing that you're not alone in this battle is a big part of winning it.

The last thing I'll mention on this is that it doesn't change when you get married. If you are a flirt before your wedding day, you will leave for your honeymoon as one. If you fail to set boundaries with the opposite sex before you marry, this will continue to be a struggle throughout your marriage. Marriage doesn't fix it; *you* must.

A word on dating

There are way too many options out there when it comes to what dating should look like. Casual dating? Courtship? Wait to date? The concept of dating didn't exist in biblical times, and the only real biblical precedent we have is arranged marriages, which most of us aren't too fired up about these days. But allow me to say just four things on the subject, and then I'll be done.

1. Take things slowly and keep things light.

I know. Easier said than done. But you must. Our tendency is to initially spend every waking moment with our new special someone. That's the example in our culture now, the consuming relationship. This tends to cloud your judgment and also alienate the rest of your friends. Even when you find the person you think is "the right one," you must still guard your heart. Spending endless amounts of time and baring your soul to one another can create a false intimacy. Genuine intimacy that lasts can only be grown slowly, over time. Set appropriate boundaries about how much time to spend together, and stick to them. And center your relationship around activities and common interests, not around your "love." In fact, I would recommend not even using the word "love" till you're ready to get engaged.

2. A word for men.

When you do decide to date someone, I believe it is appropriate for the guy to set the tone and be clear about his intentions and desires toward the woman. Even in our "enlightened" age of women's equality, I think every woman still wants to know that her guy cares enough about her to pursue her intentionally. Guys, don't make her wonder how you feel about her. And ladies, if he's unwilling to pursue you now, he certainly won't pursue you over the long haul, and he's not worth it.

3. Save the physical stuff for later.

Entire books have been written on this subject, so I will be brief. Our bodies are not meant to rev up and then stop. Which is what most couples, even Christian couples, do: they go on a romantic date, end up somewhere alone, and engage in some harmless kissing. (You're *entitled* to this, right? God doesn't expect us to be prudes, does he?) But our bodies are not happy with just kissing. Once instinct takes over, rational thinking goes out the window, and it is way too easy to get into unhealthy predicaments.

Here's the bottom line: just don't go there. It will only frustrate you. You know what's off-limits and what isn't. And it's pretty much all off-limits till your wedding night. You don't need to "try before you buy." That all takes care of itself. Set clear boundaries early in your relationship, and don't ever let the physical relationship become your focus.

4. Be accountable to a trusted friend about the relationship.

Find someone who isn't afraid to speak truth into your life, share everything with them, and then listen to what they say. Our hearts are treasures. They are valuable, to us and to God. We need to stop treating them like supermarket samples and rather embrace them as priceless treasures that must be safeguarded. Would the British government leave the crown jewels unattended for anyone to come up and take? Of course not. Likewise, we should be just as vigilant guarding our hearts. They affect *everything* we do.

A couple of years ago, one of our volunteer leaders began carving wooden hearts to give to some of our female seniors as they graduated. I stood nearby and overheard what he had to say as he gave a heart to a student. "This symbolizes your heart. It's so important. Don't just go giving it to anyone. It's too valuable for that." At one point during that student's time in college, she met a guy, things went too quickly, in essence she gave him her heart, and it got broken. She let her guard down and was greatly hurt by a guy she thought she could trust. When time came to finally end the relationship, they got together to talk, and she brought the wooden heart with her. She wanted to be able to hold onto something, to remind herself that her heart was too valuable to give away so easily.

If it helps, find a heart and put it up somewhere. (Guys, put it in a desk drawer so that you don't get made fun of.) Let it be a reminder to you that your heart is too valuable not to guard. If that doesn't work, there's always bubble wrap.

EMILY'S STORY

I grew up in a Christian home, loved going on mission trips as a teenager, and was active in my high school youth group. I didn't drink in high school, and I didn't plan on drinking in college. The summer after high school graduation, without really stopping to think about it, I started drinking heavily with my friends. Suddenly my new "normal" entailed drinking, and a few weeks later I began college. My first night on campus, my new basketball teammates wanted to drink, so I happily joined. My first weeks on campus I half-heartedly attempted to find a church in my college town, and I briefly attended the tiny on-campus ministry. But as my new partying lifestyle became more appealing, and as God-related activity only made me feel guilty about my new weekend habit, I gave up the hypocritical life I'd begun that summer and completely slipped into my new identity. I compartmentalized drinking as something I *did*, and Christian as something I *was*. I thought I'd be able to not attend church, not have a single Christian friend on campus, and still avoid becoming lost because I "knew" God. I failed, and immediately became someone I wasn't before I even realized I had lost myself. Now, *obeying* God had evaporated from my priority list, high school youth group was a distant memory, and though I occasionally read my Bible when I felt guilty and prayed when I felt sad, I never stopped to consider an alternative way of living. I made my friends, created my habits, and became an expert at ignoring Christ.

My other issue was boys. By the end of high school I was emotionally attached to my long-term boyfriend. As the only Christian in the relationship, I was solely responsible for maintaining our physical boundaries. At first I saw this as a challenge, and as a way I could "strengthen" my ability to say "no" to temptation. By my senior year, I was sick of his complaints about my boundaries and afraid he would date someone else, so I caved. I became an expert at hiding this behavior from my friends, my youth pastor, and my family. In college, I began a new cycle of relationships, becoming emotionally attached to boys who didn't understand God or my desire to follow Him, and who helped me break more and more sexual standards.

Somehow, I'd forgotten that before college I had dreamed of falling in love with a man who was so completely in love with God that he'd love me for my desire to seek Christ first. These Christ-following men, however, weren't at the parties I attended each weekend. So, because I didn't want to give up drinking, and because I was accustomed to always having someone I was either dating or pursuing, I settled for whatever boys were around. Because I refused to be the type of woman a strong Christian man would pursue, I only attracted men who pursued girls who got drunk at parties—because that was who I had become.

When graduation arrived, my situation was suddenly very different. Without friends to drink with and having been dumped by my most recent boyfriend, I was alone in a new city with a new job. I realized that I had hidden my face from God, yet wondered why I couldn't find Him. I had turned away from God, rebelled against His desire for me, and felt rejected by the One whom I'd rejected. But the choice was before me, and I had to choose: life or death? I sat up in my grave and saw the hand that God had never stopped extending. Like rebreaking a twisted bone, God had allowed the shattering of my pride and my addictions. He helped me face who I had become, and taught me to slowly, gradually, learn to believe in His grace and forgiveness.

I wish I could redo my college years, but God has shown me that *no one* is beyond salvation. I wish I had used my time in college to show others this life, rather than blending in with everyone else. By settling for what was easiest, I almost lost myself. I am blessed to know beyond a doubt that God is the only thing that is real—He is the one thing that remains. And whether we choose life or death is entirely up to us.

3.

WHAT IS A CHRISTIAN?

Anyone who knows Syler and me knows that he is a true U2 fan and I am not. Syler has all the CDs. He has videos, biographies, screen savers, and pictures from concerts. At one of our fall retreats, the worship band began an evening session with "Sunday, Bloody Sunday" with Syler coming in from the back as Bono. It was great fun, but we were all thinking, "Only Syler."

I, on the other hand, am probably not a real U2 fan. I have only two CDs. I do not know all the lyrics to even one of their songs. (To put this in context Kaila, Syler's daughter, knew almost all the words to "Elevation" at the age of three.) I can't even name all of the band members, and the ones I can, I only know their stage names. I know—pitiful.

The point here is that words like "fan" ought to mean something. And yet for this to be so, we need some clear criterion for what a "fan" is and is not. If we cannot define our labels, it is hard to show how our words and categories have much meaning.

The same is true of the label "Christian." To have a hazy understanding of what it means to be a Christian results in that title's losing its meaning and in our losing our way. Therefore, a clear definition of the name "Christian" is necessary in every generation for everyone who seeks to live by it.

In the early 1800s, Søren Kierkegaard, one of my dead friends, outlined a similar purpose to that of this chapter in the following way:

Through my writings I hope to . . . leave behind me so accurate a characterization of Christianity . . . that an enthusiastic noble-minded young person will be able to find in it a map [of authentic faith] . . . as accurate as any topographical map from the most famous institutes.

Kierkegaard saw that understanding the meaning of the title "Christian" would not only protect us from error, but would also clearly define the way forward which God has marked for us.

In Matthew 7:21–23 Jesus utters this frightening warning, "Not everyone who says to me, 'Lord, Lord,' will enter the kingdom of heaven, but only he who does the will of my Father who is in heaven. Many will say to me on that day, 'Lord, Lord, did we not prophesy in your name, and in your name drive out demon, and perform many miracles?' Then I will tell them plainly, 'I never knew you. Away from me, you evildoers.'"

Jesus is saying that there will be people who claim to be Christians (they call Jesus "Lord") and actually do miracles in his name who will be cast out of his presence because they presumed wrongly that they had authentic faith. Do you think Jesus is trying to get our attention?

The apostle Paul comes at the same point from another angle. In 2 Corinthians 13:5, as he signs off his letter he says, "Examine yourselves to see whether you are in the faith; test yourselves. Do you not realize that Christ Jesus is in you—unless of course you fail the test?" What is he getting at? He's saying the same thing as Jesus: don't presume you are a Christian. Find out what it really means and then find out if you actually are one! There is simply too much at stake to take this endeavor lightly.

In pursuit of this goal we can ask two things. First, what are a few valid definitions of "Christian" from the authority of Jesus, all of Scripture, and the whole history of the Christian church? Second, what are the absolutely essential components of the Christian faith? By seeking these most basic components, we will hopefully see its essence.

Seeking a definition

Defining something doesn't give it life, but definitions can provide the living with direction. It seems instructive to me to go back to the beginning of the faith, the time closest to Jesus himself—the writing of the New Testament, and the time when the faith was being defined in the church. Now, I realize that some of what follows here may seem elementary to some readers, but the point of this chapter is first and foremost to make sure we have these basics straight.

The name of a Christian: "Of Christ"

As we look at the history of the church, we find the word Christian showing up for the first time in Acts 11:26, "The disciples were called Christians first in Antioch." The name Christian simply means "of Christ," or a follower of Christ. This word is derived much like the label "Herodians" (a group mentioned in the Gospels) since they are "of Herod," that is, loyalists or followers of King Herod.

The meaning of discipleship

The meaning of being a Christ follower is fleshed out further in Jesus's call to "discipleship," which is simply his call for those interested in following him. The invitation to discipleship is a call to have so much faith in Jesus that one accepts his or her place as his unconditional student and obedient servant. In this way, one definition of "Christian" is simply to be Christ's disciple—to be "of Christ."[2]

However, being Christ's disciple should not be confused with accepting Jesus on our own terms. To be a disciple in the ancient world (and of course the New Testament uses the word "disciple" in this context) is to take the whole of the teacher and his philosophy, and to obey the teacher as a master. So then, to be Christ's disciple is first to accept the center of his teaching, his own divinity, which is therefore also to accept that we will always be disciples.

The depth of discipleship

Further, discipleship (being "of Christ") is to follow Jesus without limitation or reserve. Jesus makes this clear in his own definition of discipleship in Luke 9:23, "If anyone wants to come after me, he must deny himself and take up his cross daily and follow me." Here there is no reservation. There is no fallback option. The commitment Jesus seeks from us is daily and to the point of taking up, or accepting the fate of, a cross—the great Roman instrument of torture and death.

Jesus calls for a daily commitment of unconditional surrender to follow him wherever he leads, yet his mention of the cross is meant to remind you that you have not been called to anything he was not willing to face himself. This is why Romans 8:16-17 promises to Christians, ". . . we are children of God, and if children, heirs also, heirs of God and fellow heirs with Christ, *if indeed we suffer with him so that we may also be glorified with him* (NASB). "

---

2. Some have argued that one can be a Christian "believer" and yet not be a "disciple." It is my understanding that to believe this is to make up categories that do not exist. In the New Testament, discipleship and faith (becoming a believer) are synonymous.

The position of a Christian: "In Christ"

If being named Christian makes one "of Christ," then being a Christian can also be defined by our position "in Christ." As the apostle Paul explains our relationship to Christ in his New Testament letters, he uses the phrase "in Christ" almost ninety times in a variety of ways, all of which create a picture of genuine Christian faith.

Our legal position in Christ: Justification

Paul says that a Christian's faith is "in Christ." A Christian is a person who has put the weight of her trust on the person of Jesus, and specifically in the rescuing power of his death. She has accepted that she has offended the God of the universe with her sin, and has accepted that the anger of God against us is not because he is uptight but because we are insolent. Having accepted this, she is in a state of condemnation, being helpless to save herself, and she therefore places her trust in the cross of Jesus to make atonement for her sins. Her sin is punished in the death of Jesus, and God credits Christ's righteousness (or completely spotless moral cleanness) to her (2 Cor. 5:17–19, Gal. 2:16, Phil. 3:9).

This result of putting one's faith in Christ, also called "justification," is like the door entering into the house of the family of God. This is not the end and total of being a Christian, but the New Testament makes it clear that no one can be a Christian without being justified through faith in Jesus.

Our social situation in Christ: The church

Although justification is the door into the family of God, it is not the whole house. Now, having put our faith in Christ, we actually become "in Christ" in two ways. First, we become children of God very literally by means of adoption. John 1:12 says, "Yet to all who received him [Jesus], to those who believed in his name, *he gave the right to become children of God."* This right extends to all who have come to faith in Christ. Second, this faith unites all people who have entered into Christ's family. Paul makes much of this in Galatians 3:26–29:

> You are all *sons of God* through faith in Christ Jesus, for all of you who were baptized into Christ have clothed yourselves with Christ. There is neither Jew nor Greek, slave nor free, male nor female, for you *are all one* in Christ Jesus. If you belong to Christ, then you are Abraham's seed, and heirs according to the promise.

Anyone who is in Christ is therefore an equal part of God's family. It is a family that sees our unity in Christ as each person's defining feature and not their race, age, sex, customs, or class. Although everyone brings different strengths and weaknesses to the table, we have all come to the same family, with the same Father, in the same way.

The Bible simply calls this new family the church. It is a body of people that spans history and geography and is assigned to do God's work on earth. It is not something you can choose to join after you come to faith. If you come to Christ, you become part of his family by definition. If the church has problems, they're family problems—your family problems. Reform, not escape and blame, is our calling.

Our mystical experience in Christ: Christ in us

Paul's most persistent use of the phrase "in Christ" is to refer to the means, or the reason why the Father does something. He freely gives us many things, not because we are so loveable, but because he does it "in Christ" or, because of our new relationship to Christ. Yet of all the many things God gives us, the most stunning thing he gives us "in Christ," or because of Christ, is *himself.* God is the greatest and most fulfilling gift God has for us, and much religious disappointment comes from missing this fact. Therefore we cannot discuss our being "in Christ" without accepting the mystical presence of Christ constantly with us in the person of the Holy Spirit.

The Bible promises us that to have Christ is to have God, the Holy Spirit, in us. In John 14:16–17 Jesus says, "I will ask the Father, and he will give you another Counselor to be with you forever—the Spirit of truth. The world cannot accept him, because it neither sees him nor knows him. But you know him, for he lives with you and will be in you."

Here Jesus makes clear that the Holy Spirit was to live with and even in his followers, and this gift of the Holy Spirit was going to come from the Father because of the cross work of Jesus, or we might say "in Christ."

It is hard to overestimate the importance of this union for the Christian. It is because of this Spirit that we have come to Christ. It is through him that we have a transformed spirit with new God-oriented desires (historically called "regeneration"). It is through the same Spirit that God reveals himself to our intellect and emotions so we can appreciate and enjoy him. And it is this same Spirit who helps us to live a holy life, no longer a slave to sin (historically called "sanctification").

There is an enormous amount that can be said about the presence of God within the Christian, but for the sake of definition we need only say that God's immediate presence is part of the New Testament definition of essential Christianity.

The essentials: Necessary components for biblical Christianity

Above we have looked at two definitions for what it means to be a Christian: that we are both "of Christ" and "in Christ." However, this does not get to the very essentials. What are the absolutely essential components we must hold to be personally assured that we are Christians and rightly sharing God's message with others? I see three major essentials: having faith in Jesus, living in love, and persevering in hope. Although it may be possible to be a Christian and not know or believe every point I will mention below, I see these as the big themes and emphases that God has revealed in Christ and in the pages of Scripture.

Essential one: Faith in Jesus

First, a Christian must have *faith* in *Jesus*. First Jesus. God went through an unbelievable amount of trouble to communicate himself to us accurately through his revelation to us in Jesus Christ. Hebrews 1:3 says, "The Son is the radiance of God's glory and the exact representation of his being." God is serious about our worshiping him for who he is and not who we make him up to be. He calls the latter "idolatry." So, if you are going to have faith in Jesus, you've got to have faith in the Jesus of history, the Jesus of the Bible, the Jesus who really was and really is. If we make up the Jesus we're going to believe in—a nice, soft, tame Jesus—we will be idolaters, not Christians.

Now faith. We need to understand that in the Bible, faith is expressed through words and actions. God is the one who popularized the notion that actions speak louder than words. That is why we can be saved by faith and judged by works, because God sees our words as authentic or inauthentic, based on the reality of our lives. Faith, then, is not merely making a statement that we accept Jesus, but is having a constant trust in Christ's provision and direction that transforms us from the inside out.

Essential two: A life of love

The second absolute essential is a life of love. In 1 Corinthians 13:1–3 the apostle Paul says:

> If I speak in the tongues of men and of angels, but have not love, I am only a resounding gong or a clanging cymbal. If I have the gift of prophecy and can fathom all mysteries and all knowledge, and if I have a faith that can move mountains, but have not love, I am nothing. If I give all I possess to the poor and surrender my body to the flames, but have not love, I gain nothing.

That's pretty powerful stuff.

Yet Jesus makes just as potent a statement in John 13:34–35, "A new command I give you: Love one another. As I have loved you, so you must love one another. By this all men will know that you are my disciples, if you love one another." Both of these statements are astonishing. Paul claims that if he is not a person of love, even if he is a miracle worker, he is nothing. Nor are his prophecies or the depth of his theology worth anything without love.

Jesus also banks everything on this life-transforming, self-sacrificing lifestyle. "*As I have loved you*, so you must love one another." He first makes sure we are not going to fall for some nonsensical, media-driven definition of love. He did this by binding love's definition to his own life, and then makes it the main criterion by which the watching world will know whether we are really his disciples or not. Christianity in one sense is a life of love. But it is love that is motivated by the Father's gift, empowered by the Holy Spirit, and defined by Jesus's life, and especially his death.

Essential three: Perseverance in hope

Last is the fact that we have to finish. We have to *become* Christians (come to faith), *be* Christians (live in love), and finally *die* Christians (persevere in hope). Although making it to the end is critical in Scripture, this essential has not always been well appreciated. There have been many who have wanted to say that merely "accepting Jesus" sincerely allows anyone to gain eternal life, which cannot be lost. They have claimed that God accepts all those who have sincere faith in Jesus at any point in life, and he does not give and then snatch away his eternal life. "Once saved, always saved." What happens in a person's life after their initial commitment is really irrelevant to her eternal destiny. From one momentary act of faith, their sins are forgiven and they are permanently and irrevocably saved.

As I understand the New Testament, this is foreign to everything the Bible says faith is. John Wesley used to say that this doctrine "sent men to hell with smiles on their faces" and caused people to think that they didn't have to be holy in order to be Christian.[3] The New Testament assumes everywhere that holiness and persistence in faith are essential parts of Christianity. Colossians 1:22-23 says we are presented to God without blemish and free from accusation "*if* you continue . . . established and firm, not moved from the hope held out in the gospel." Yet this and many other passages aside, I think the clearest statement concerning the necessity for perseverance is in the book of Revelation.

Eight times in the book of Revelation, John records Christ's glorious promise of ultimate salvation to the one "who overcomes. . . ." This promise is astounding. The one who overcomes will not be hurt by God's final judgment, and Jesus promises that such a person "will sit on my throne." And then, after a powerful description of the everlasting heavenly city, Jesus says that the one who overcomes "will inherit all this."[4]

This is a serious promise, but it is not promised to the one who "signed a decision card" or "made a really sincere profession of faith at one point." It doesn't even matter if you cried a lot. What matters is that you make it.

So Nic, what happens to assurance? Doesn't God want me to know that I'm accepted and saved? Yes and no. The Bible says that if you have come to faith, you are in the faith. Yet the Bible only offers us assurance while we are on the path. 1 John 2:5b-6 says, "This is how we know we are in him: whoever claims to live in him *must walk as Jesus did.*" Colossians 4:12 says, "that you may *stand firm in all the will of God,* mature and *fully assured.*" Our assurance comes from the present, telling us our past conversion was real and giving us a hope in the future arrival of the Risen Jesus and the full presence of the Kingdom of God.

---

3. The theological word for this is "antinomianism," literally "against the law."

4. To do a quick study of these promises in Revelation, see the following verses: 2:7, 2:11, 2:17, 2:26, 3:5, 3:12, 3:21, and 21:7.

The question we must ask ourselves to seek assurance in our faith is: Am I serving Jesus right now? Do I love the cross now? Am I trusting Christ today for forgiveness and strength? Am I, to the best of my knowledge, living this minute in the will of God? If you can answer in truth, Yes, then you are indeed standing firm, mature, and fully assured. We must persevere, and we must find the motivation to do so in the hope of glory, so that some day we can say with Paul, "I have fought the good fight, I have *finished the race*, I have kept the faith" (2 Tim. 4:7).

So what? A few applications

So what do we do with this? First, ask yourself if you are a Christian right now. Have you carefully considered what the Christian life really is? Are you really in? You must confirm this every day. This doesn't mean you "get saved" each day, but simply that you choose for each day that you want to follow Jesus and that you have justifying faith in Christ.

Second, is your understanding of God small, self-centered, and basically a bunch of idolatry? You will not be happy in God until you grow out of this. Playing church will not last.

Third, there is no true conversion without discipleship. If a transformed life, deep love, and perseverance are Christian essentials, then conversion is not the be-all-end-all. If living as Christ's disciple is God's race and those who are not Christians are spectators, then success for us is not only in crossing the starting line but making it to the end. We cannot only start the race, but we need to run it well and finish it strong.

Last, and related to the third point, living for Christ involves accepting his plan and his way. Christ's plan is the church. Many of my students know I love the book *The Lord of the Rings*. I find that many devout young Christians are like Strider the ranger. Strider is a man of the wilds. He can make it on his own. He anticipates danger, knows all the healing herbs, and is the most cunning warrior known with a bow or sword. But the story is not about how he becomes skillful as a warrior; the story is about how he becomes great as a man. And that greatness comes when he gives up his perfect solitary freedom to throw his lot in with the imperfect world of men as they face a common enemy. Accepting responsibility, even unwanted responsibility, obediently takes a peculiar kind of bravery.

Just as Strider did not want to be involved in the affairs or battles of men, so many young Christians do not want to be involved in the affairs of the church, or more specifically, any local church. Independence and freedom seem more attractive, and the church seems so obsolete, so defective. G.K. Chesterton said that when we think like this, we are like people who constantly proclaim to love mankind but are incapable of loving our neighbor.

But God has appointed the church, and specifically, local churches as God's plan for our making it in his way. You cannot lead a great Christian life outside the fellowship of the church. The Bible knows nothing of solo Christianity. Its main virtue is one that cannot be done alone—love—and its object is the salvation of all people.

We need each other to make it. You've heard "no man is an island," but maybe you didn't know that the phrase comes from a pastor (John Donne), and that he got the concept from Jesus. We need corunners to live our everyday lives; we need Christian peers to encourage us and hold our feet to the fire. We need coaches (pastors and teachers) to help us run better. And we need heroes of the faith to inspire us to be great and to show us what greatness really looks like. There are a hundred common goals that we cannot achieve alone. One well-known church adopted the saying, "we came together to do what none of us could do alone." Perfect.

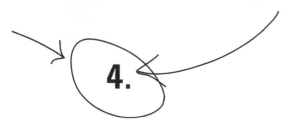

DEALING WITH DOUBT

Chances are, if you're reading this book, following Jesus matters a whole lot to you. And if you've made it this far in the book, there's also a very good chance that not only are you a "Christian," but also you're the kind of Christian that would like to see your relationship with God grow each day and month and year. You're not just in this for Grandma Betty's Jell-O molds on potluck night; God has gotten hold of your heart, and you deeply desire to serve him with your whole life. Many of the students we youth pastors send into the "real world" have this same desire. But in too many instances, somewhere along the way their desire to remain committed to God gets derailed.

When I was a freshman, it was downright depressing how many of my Christian friends had left their faith behind by the end of the year. It is not uncommon for many college students to go through a phase known as the "Dark Night of the Soul," where they question everything they've known to be true up to that point. It can be an extremely scary time. The irony, though, is that the very thing that has the potential to kill your faith also has the potential to take it to the next level. When counseling committed Christians who are experiencing doubt, pastor and author Brian McLaren first tells them that doubt is not always bad. "In fact, sometimes doubt is absolutely essential. Doubt is like pain: it tells us that something nearby or within us is dangerous. It calls for attention and action." My hope in this chapter is to help you prepare for your times of doubt so that doubt is a faith-building rather than a faith-maiming experience.

Why doubt is good

One of the worst things you can believe about being a Christian is that doubting equals sinning. This is simply not true. In fact, I think that the poor apostle with the first name of Doubting (and a really cool last name) gets a bad rap in the church. It's as though people blame him for not having enough faith. Guess what? I would have done the same thing. They've just been abandoned by their leader of three years—sure, he told him this was coming, but he was always speaking in parables. Who knew that he really meant it when he said he would die? And as of Saturday night, there was still no sign that Jesus was anywhere but rotting in his tomb. Thomas was simply being honest about the doubts in his heart, and so should we.

Doubting is not dangerous; in fact, it is often a sign that you are moving to a deeper level in your faith. Think of your faith like sedimentary rock. Each layer builds on the next, and the layer beneath forms the foundation for the next layer until you have a beautiful piece of rock.

Or imagine your faith like the houses of the three little pigs. The first house you build is made out of straw. It's a functioning house, but all it takes is a little huffin' and puffin' and it comes down. This is the point where many young Christians walk away. They say: Look, if this God thing was real, my house would still be standing. The other alternative is to say: You know, the house of faith that I was building was adequate for a time, but it's not strong enough anymore. I need to build a stronger house, with a firmer foundation and better materials. And so you build again, this time out of sticks. It's a better house, but it might take four or five puffs to bring it down.

You are once again at a pivotal time, and you can either leave the house destroyed or build another one, this time out of bricks. You learn from your mistakes, and the newer understanding of God that you find each time your previous house gets blown to the ground brings the wisdom to build a better house the next time. Let's take a look at a few of the ways that doubt can appear.

Doubt from poor decisions

First, doubt can sometimes enter our lives simply as a result of our own foolish decisions. Tony Campolo relates how he responded to a certain Christian college student who came into his office to talk about his doubts. Tony asked him: How long have you been shacking up with your girlfriend? Sure enough, Tony had read the situation accurately. The student knew what he was doing was wrong, but didn't want to stop, so he was walking away from the God who he believed was restricting him.

If you are simply enjoying your sin too much to stop, you will find it difficult to have a strong, vibrant faith. Others of you may have a genuine desire to follow God, but because your struggle against sin is getting the best of you, you doubt that He is real because your struggle is too intense.

Something you should keep in mind if you're in this category is that as a newer Christian, you are not yet fully the person that God wants you to be. While it's true that as a follower of Jesus you are a new creature, that doesn't mean that you automatically start behaving like one. The following diagram helps to explain the journey that you're on in relationship to your outward behavior.

Many of us think the Christian life is like this:

We read in 2 Corinthians 5:17 about how when we come to Christ we are new creations, and we think: OK, I'm a new creation, so my struggle with sin should be long gone. I was heading toward hell, but now I'm heading toward heaven, so why do I still struggle? You struggle because it's a whole lot more complicated than that.

What I've noticed in my own life is that the Christian life looks more like this:

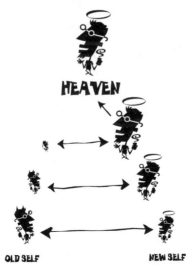

Early on, for many of you, there will be a big gap between your "Christian self" and your "worldly self." Sometimes you feel like two completely different people, depending on who's around. Other days you feel like you're moving closer toward heaven, and on some days you feel like you're moving backward. But as your faith grows, that gap narrows, as does the influence your "worldly self" has on your life. It never completely disappears, but there will come a time when you feel as though you are the same consistent person in all circumstances.

You must give yourself the grace God wants to give you until your spiritual maturity catches up with your desire to please him. Even a mature Christian like Paul confessed his own struggles with sin in Romans:

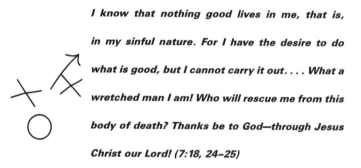

I know that nothing good lives in me, that is, in my sinful nature. For I have the desire to do what is good, but I cannot carry it out. . . . What a wretched man I am! Who will rescue me from this body of death? Thanks be to God—through Jesus Christ our Lord! (7:18, 24–25)

So while our decisions can increase doubt, our steps toward spiritual maturity can strengthen our faith.

Doubt from suffering

Times of personal suffering or tragedy can often bring doubt. When I was a senior in college, things could not have been better. I had just begun dating Heidi, my wife. We had just started the InterVarsity chapter at our school, we were seeing new people come to faith, and our small group of Christians was praying together regularly. It was an exciting time, and my faith seemed stronger than it had ever been. Everything fell apart when Heidi's mom was fatally injured in an ice skating accident. Absolutely nothing could have prepared me for dealing with the aftermath of that event. As the strong encourager that I thought I could be to Heidi, I would often say things like, "We're going to get through this; God is going to get us through." However, to her they were just empty words. If God really loved her, why would He take away the person that meant the most to her?

The next two years were extremely challenging and were often filled with lingering doubts. It felt like we were forced to grow up a lot faster than we wanted to. To this day, we can't say that we are happy for what happened. But we were faced with the choice of either believing that God is in control or He isn't, either that He is good or He isn't. We chose to believe Scripture's truth: that He's both in control and good, in spite of the pain that His Providence sometimes brings. We took the rubble of the easy-answer faith that had crumbled, brushed it aside, and went to work building our next "house of faith" out of stronger materials than before.

What we learned during that time is something that Christians in all time periods have noted and that the Bible makes clear: life in general, and specifically a life of following Jesus, is hard and full of suffering, not pleasure. A poem written by John Piper expresses the biblical concept of what he calls God's sustaining grace:

Not grace to bar what is not bliss

Nor flight from all distress, but this:

A grace that orders our trouble and pain

And then, in the darkness, is there to sustain[5]

5. Sermon from 1996 entitled "Sustaining Grace."

God's grace is not there to shield us from difficulty, and it does not instruct us to run away from suffering. Rather, it is a sovereign grace that guides and directs our trouble, and then sustains us in the midst of it.

When doubts come because of suffering, the natural thing to do is to shake your fist at God. Yes, as the one who is in control of all events, He does allow the pain. But He's also the only one to whom we can turn to receive sustaining comfort. In the Psalms, we see modeled for us the example of an honest prayer life before God. In Psalm 6, David cries out in great distress, "My soul is in anguish. How long, O Lord, how long?" (v. 3). In Psalm 73, Asaph wrestles with the concept of the justice of God: how can good things keep happening to wicked people? Few of our worship meetings reflect the real pain and confusion found in the Bible's own songbook. Yet consistently, the psalmists come to the same conclusion: life is hard, but God is good. In the very next verse of Psalm 6, David says, "Turn, O Lord, and deliver me; save me because of your unfailing love" (v. 4). In spite of his anguish and frustration, he knows that he can find his deliverance in one place only: in the loving arms of a merciful God.

Nickel Creek's song "Reasons Why" describes a person whose faith has slowly eroded.

Where am I today? I wish that I knew

Cause looking around there's no sign of you

I don't remember one jump or one leap

Just quiet steps away from your lead

We get distracted by dreams of our own

But nobody's happy while feeling alone

And knowing how hard it hurts when we fall

We lean another ladder against the wrong wall

And climb high to the highest rung,

to shake fists at the sky. . . .[6]

A walk away from God often happens slowly rather than in an instant. Before you know it, you believe that "God has left you," while the reality is that you have taken the small, quiet steps away from God. The final line of the song expresses the disillusionment that can come from a challenging life: "With so much deception, it's hard not to wander away." And we shake our fists at the only one who can truly comfort us. It's OK to be honest about your doubt and disillusionment. It's OK to take a step back to question what you believe. But be careful that your "little break" doesn't turn into totally abandoning God.

Doubt from intellectual challenges

There are also intellectual challenges to be faced. Nic addresses several of these in his chapter on relativism, but let me briefly say here that you need to be prepared for the assault your faith will take, especially in any religion and philosophy classes you take at a secular university. Be prepared to be called closed-minded, intolerant, and judgmental.

One of my greatest faith struggles came in a comparative religions class I took. We spent a good deal of time studying Native American religions and read a book about one religious leader named Black Elk, an Oglala Sioux. The book chronicled the messages Black Elk was receiving from the Great Spirit, which promised him that if he followed all of his commands, the Wasichu (white men) would be

---

6. Chris Thile, Sean Watkins, and David Puckett, *Reasons Why: The Very Best,* Sugar Hill, 2006.

defeated and his people would be restored. While I was reading, I was struck for the first time in my life with the notion of a person from another religion who seemed to be receiving messages from God that had nothing to do with Jesus. I thought: perhaps God would communicate His truth to different people in different ways. This shook me up a great deal.

Fortunately, unlike other books I read in high school and college, I read this one all the way to the end! The end of the story proved that the messages were not, in fact, divine. Black Elk's people are defeated and the messages he had been receiving were proved false. Here's how the book ends: "And I, to whom so great a vision was given in my youth, you see me now a pitiful old man who has done nothing, for the nation's hoop is broken and scattered. There is no center any longer, and the sacred tree is dead."[7] Tragically, this man had been deceived.

Now I learned from this experience a couple things. First of all, studying other religions and viewpoints is an invaluable experience. We can't *only* study Christianity and assume that everyone else is wrong. Everything you discover to be true is ultimately from God, whether it's "Christian" or not. But I also learned that there is something truly unique about Christianity and about Jesus himself. As Paul says in Colossians 2:9, "in Christ all the fullness of the Deity lives in bodily form." The *fullness* of God doesn't dwell in anyone else. While there may be a lot wrong with the way Christianity is played out in the church today, Jesus hasn't changed, and he's still our hope. Many of you will likely encounter a similar struggle I faced, depending on your situation. And you will have to decide for yourself what you believe.

Don't ever think that you have to turn off your brain or your reason when it comes to Christianity. It has stood up to over two thousand years of opposition; Yahweh can handle your intellectual questions.

7. John Neihardt, *Black Elk Speaks* (Lincoln: University of Nebraska Press, 1932), 270.

You may not like the answer when you find it, but much of the journey comes in asking the questions. Don't shy away from these challenges; rather, stare them in the face, ask the hard questions, and seek wise counsel from those who won't give you cliché answers. Go to the Bible and to other good literature that can offer insight. This is what college should be all about: wrestling with the hard questions. Say to the questions what Jacob said to the angel: I will not let you go until you bless me. The way out is not *around*, but *through* the heart of your questions.

Doubt from disappointment

Finally, when circumstances or friends disappoint us, our faith can wither and die. It's easy to put others on a pedestal, especially Christians we respect. We can almost worship them rather than God. My earliest mentor and high school youth group leader walked away from the faith while I was still in high school and to my knowledge has not returned. People that you think are invincible and perfect will fail you. The words of Micah are appropriate here: "Do not trust a neighbor; put no confidence in a friend. . . . But as for me, I watch in hope for the LORD, I wait for God my Savior; my God will hear me" (7:5, 7). On one hand, it is appropriate to follow the example of trusted mentors, just as Paul says to follow him as he follows Christ (1 Cor. 11:1). On the other hand, we should always hope first in the Triune God, who will never disappoint us.

To close, I want to share a practical word about walking through a time of doubt. There's a difference between experiencing doubt inside the safety of the church community and outside of it. It's wrong to assume that you're no longer a Christian just because you go through a phase of doubting, and to think that you must then leave the community as a result. As I've said, this can be a very fruitful and growing time, especially if it's done in the context of a healthy community. When you decide to leave the community, you open yourself up to the added danger of sin. And a time of doubt plus a desire to sin can lead to a long walk away from God, rather than a short time of wrestling with Him.

In the book of Mark, after Jesus heals a boy with an evil spirit, his father says this: "I do believe; help me overcome my unbelief!" (9:24). Jesus doesn't rebuke him. I find great comfort in those words. We walk through a challenging world faced with all sorts of questions, but Jesus just asks for a mustard seed-sized faith, and a heart that wants that faith to grow. It is not a question of if, but when doubts will come. When they do, let your house fall to the ground, confident that God will be there to help you rebuild.

RAY'S STORY

I went into college as a pretty new Christian with a serious case of thinking I was the best thing to ever drop his knees at the altar. I had become a Christian completely accidentally halfway through high school, after a fair amount of recreational drug use. I had no Christian friends to speak of in high school, and I was not a part of a Christian family, so my only fellowship happened in a weekly "stop by" at my youth pastor's office. Needless to say, my number one goal in transitioning to college was to find Christians who I could be friends with. I wanted some real friends and maybe one older wise mentor figure, but mostly people my same age who wanted to serve God in the same way I did.

Lucky for me I went to a big Christian school where I quickly made more Christian friends than I knew what to do with. My main group of friends came from a big church near campus that I jumped into faster than I could think straight. At the church I was taken in as somebody with potential to become a leader. I bought into these expectations not as a humble servant excited to serve God in whatever capacity He had for me, but in anticipation of the admiration I would receive from people as I continued to move up in leadership. As my momentum grew, so did my bitterness toward the church that was creating it. My first ever college mentor decided that we had to end our relationship because I was not willing to commit to being a small group leader by the middle of my sophomore year. I was expected to share my faith in ways that I was uncomfortable with, and not given answers to questions that I felt were important to consider. All in all, by the end of my sophomore year, I had a million Christian friends that I did not want to talk to ever again. I was burnt out on church, "community," and on any outward display of faith (though my inward faith was still very much alive).

Here's the kicker: I was honest about it. I told everybody what I was going through. Ultimately, about half of my vast network of friends estranged themselves from me. It didn't hurt as bad as I thought it would. My "community" had changed from a huge network of people who I only knew through surface level conversations to a smaller group of people who I grew to know deeply. The next year was spent enjoying the fruit of this close-knit community of which I had become a part. It was also spent pushing a few moral boundaries that I previously viewed as deplorable for a Christian to explore. It wasn't that I was questioning my faith during this time; in fact, I had never been more serious about it. I led an inner-city ministry for fifth- and sixth-graders, and I started attending a church where homeless people and college students could all worship together free of judgment. I am by no means condoning my moral-boundary pushing, but during that time I realized that meeting Christ did not start and end with behavioral modification. Meeting Christ starts with realizing His love for you and for the rest of humanity and acting in a way that displays that love.

Senior year was the test of that previous statement. I started my work with the poor being moved by love, and in my last year of college I used it as an excuse to assume that I was always "okay." My drinking increased when I became legal, but my level of honesty and intimacy with my "community" increased with it. Without going into too many details, I lost control of myself. My close friends, who were all church-going Christians, lost control of themselves with me. Here I learned the next lesson in community: be aware of when your community is failing you. All of my close friends from college are still my closest friends, but what we really needed was an older, wiser Christian to come in and separate the good from the bad parts of our lives. Our honesty, closeness, and encouragement were not enough because they were not centered on God. They were centered on ourselves. We learned that love outside of God quickly turns into a selfish love if not checked by wisdom. I had come full circle. I had made Christian friends, then rebelled against strict boundaries that people had put on me, only to run straight into the opposite problem of a life with no boundaries. Now being in the midst of my third year in the "real world," I've learned more and more that part of being a Christian is realizing when you've fallen and not being afraid to look for who is there to help you up.

INTERACTING WITH SCRIPTURE

Almost every Christian struggles with consistently reading the Bible and praying. Even though Paul states emphatically in 2 Timothy 3:16–17, "All Scripture is God-breathed and is useful" so we can be "thoroughly equipped for every good work," many Christians still ignore their Bible as the urgent and easy tasks of the day take all of their attention.

I won't scare you with the number of *pastors* who hardly even read the Bible or pray. You'd be floored. Pastors or not, though we think highly of the Bible, we don't seem to think highly enough of it to seriously and habitually read it.

One of the reasons for this is that when we come to the Bible, we do it in unhelpful ways. It is common to think that the Bible will be light, inspirational reading. It is not. Sometimes people think that the verses of the Bible are like allergy medication—just take one daily and you'll be in perfect health. They are not. Others freely associate whatever they read with the personal experiences they are having at that moment. This person might be stressing over an exam and read Matthew 3:1–4 where people go out into the desert to meet with John the Baptist. He may take from this that he needs to go out into the woods in order to really get away and seek God in this stressful time. That may be a helpful spiritual exercise, but it is an unhelpful way of interpreting the Scriptures.

The Holy Scriptures in the Christian life

I have two purposes in this chapter. First, I want to convince you that you *must* read the Bible. My unashamed goal is to make you excited about the life change that will come from reading and obeying God's word. I want you to feel the sense of duty you have as Christ's ambassador to a world ignorant of his message, and I want you to feel deeply afraid that you could be the "fool" in Scripture that does not meditate on the law of God and is led astray into the enemy's deadly trap (Ps. 1).

Second, I want to answer the question, "How should I read and study the Bible?" I want to give a few guidelines for interpretation and reading, and then simply encourage you that the diamond mining of studying the Scriptures is worth the hard work.

Finding the motivation

So then, if you must read the Bible, where do you find the motivation necessary to meaningfully and consistently do it? First, *let yourself be motivated by love for God.* Do you love Jesus Christ? This book is *His* word, *His* instruction. It is the repetition of *His* encouragement, and the vocalization of *His* love for you. *He* is teaching you about how *He* feels and thinks about you, and is sharing His heart with you. If you love Him now, how much more will that be so when your knowledge of Him deepens? Further, the Scriptures teach us *how* to love Him. Do you want to express your love passionately, yet appropriately? Expressions of love always require knowing the person being loved, and the Bible will tutor you in loving Christ. Reading the Bible will increase and reawaken your love for your Savior and King.

Second, *let yourself be motivated by the honorable sense of duty you feel as a member of God's country,* "The Kingdom of Heaven" as Jesus called it. Hebrews 12:1 says, "Therefore, since we are surrounded by such a great cloud of witnesses, let us throw off everything that hinders and the sin that so easily entangles, and let us run with perseverance the race marked out for us." Do you see the picture? Every believer who has ever lived is part of a huge epic story. God has given his people the task of drawing all nations into his kingdom through faith and obedience to Christ. Christ has gone before us and completed his part. Twenty centuries of faithful men and women have gone before us, living and dying to fulfill God's plan. Now it is our turn.

Listen, Paul is *dead.* Augustine is *dead.* Jerome, Gregory the Great, Anselm, Francis of Assisi, Luther, Calvin, Teresa of Avila, Edwards, Whitefield, Wesley, Seraphim of Sarov, Newman, Moody, and all these heroes have gone the way of all flesh. Yes, they've been reborn to heaven but the race has been passed on to *us* and it is *our* turn to run. Do you feel the honor and weight of your place in history? Are you motivated by a sense of duty, knowing that there is a company in heaven along with Christ Himself cheering you on to run well in your lifetime?

Now I have to ask, how will you run well without training? How will you fight the battle without first learning how to fight? How will you teach others truth and unravel lies if you remain a novice all your life? We are motivated first by our love for Jesus, but we must also be motivated by the honor of fulfilling our Christ-appointed duty in the kingdom of heaven, and by the shame that will come if we leave our task undone.

Finally, *let yourself also be motivated by fear of falling away from Christ and coming under the judgment of God.* Some fear makes you a slave, but this fear can save your life. Hear the warning of 2 Peter 2:20: "If they have escaped the corruption of the world by knowing our Lord and Savior Jesus Christ and *are again entangled in it and overcome, they are worse off at the end than they were at the beginning.*" The warning: you have to make it to the end. You have to *finish* the race. There is a sinfulness in the world and in you that wants you to be its slave—it wants to *overcome* you, but there is a new voice of righteousness in you through the Holy Spirit calling *you to overcome* everything that stands in opposition to the kingdom of heaven.

You don't need to be discouraged. God has given you everything you need to succeed. He has chosen you to be His, called you and expressed His love for you in Christ's death and the Holy Spirit's presence. He has promised that nothing and no one from the outside can snatch you away from His care (Jn. 10, Rom. 8). He has given you everything you need to win: power, encouragement, advice, training, love, help, and companions. However, *He has seen fit that you would learn how to use all of these advantages by studying and applying his Word.* Through the *Bible* He declares His love for you. Through the *Bible* He warns you of the enemy's sneak attacks. Through the *Bible* He teaches wisdom. You get the point.

This does not by any means negate the importance of pastoral preaching, church commitment, Christian community, spiritual disciplines, or prayer. It *is* to say that the Bible is the manual to take full advantage of and to test all of these things. So now allow your *theology* to form a *conviction to motivate* you to study the Scriptures out of a passionate love, an honorable duty, and a liberating fear.

Reading and studying the Bible

I need to say three things about reading and studying the Bible.

1. Bible passages have one meaning.[8]

   2. That meaning is controlled by the context the passage is in.

   3. Sometimes you have to dig and fight to find it.

That's not rocket science, but it's amazing how many people don't really understand or apply these three simple points.

First, *Bible passages have one meaning, or are getting at one main truth.* Obviously, godly men and women will disagree some-times on what that meaning is, but my purpose is to contrast this with interpretation styles primarily interested in what "this passage means to me." If you have not encountered a group (or individual—maybe yourself) that functions on this model already, you probably will in college.

Participants in this view reflect on a passage of Scripture and share whatever comes to mind. All answers are typically offered as what this passage "means to me," and there is positive affirma-tion even to contradictory opinions. The insight of J.P. Moreland on this point is instructive:

"Over the years this creates a feeling of safety in the [group], but at the price of generating both a false sense of pride and the mistaken notion that all opinions are equal, whether

---

8. By "one meaning" I mean that the biblical author of a passage had something specific in mind when writing it. That does not mean it has only one "significance" or only one application. The reason I speak here about the single meaning of the text is because we need to do the work of finding that meaning before we start assessing its present significance and applying it to our lives.

spontaneously and quickly conceived or the result of detailed study prior to [group] time. It also keeps [people] from learning how to receive criticism for their ideas in the interest of truth and stifles growth in our ability to [not respond to such criticism defensively]." [9]

The point here is that the *Bible* is saying something, not your psyche. It is saying the same thing to you as it has said to all of its readers in all generations. It is calling you a sinner. It is teaching you wisdom and calling you to obedience. It is expressing God's love. If we put our conscious or subconscious thoughts on the passages we read, and don't ask intently, "What is this passage trying to tell me?" Scripture will not change us. In this way, the question "What are you saying to *me, Lord*?" concerning 1 Corinthians 1:11–19 (for example) must come through the question, "What is *Paul* saying to the *Corinthians*?" When we realize that we, just like the Corinthians, are human, sinful, and in need of Christ's power and teaching, we realize we do not need to learn a "deeper" or "more modern" lesson than they did, but the same one Paul was teaching them.

This brings us to our second point: *each text's meaning is determined and controlled by its context.*[10] Bible scholars usually call this a "grammatical-historical exegesis," which simply means that God is speaking through the Bible's human authors using the normal rules of language and in a particular historical context. Therefore, we have to first understand the language and the

9. J.P. Moreland, *Love Your God with All Your Mind* (Colorado Springs, CO: Navpress, 1997), 97.
10. A "text" in this context refers to a piece of Scripture as small as one verse or as large as the whole Bible.

context of a passage in order to understand God's timeless message in the text.

Understanding what the biblical author is saying in the historical context is what is called "exegesis" (pronounced "ex-uh-JEE-sis" in case you want to impress your friends at your next Bible study) and then applying that truth in today's context is called "hermeneutics." The point of distinguishing these two parts is to say: don't try to do skip to application (hermeneutics) before you do the hard work of analysis (exegesis). Remember that God is saying something in the passage. It may not be what you want to hear at that moment, but chances are it is what you *need* to hear.

Finally, *getting God's message out of the Bible,* understanding it with clarity, and applying it to your life can be hard work. Not only that, it can also be painful. You've probably heard of Martin Luther. He referred to the hard work of interpreting the book of Romans as "beating upon Paul." The clear inspired message was there to be dug out. We too have to be prepared to beat on these passages with our minds until the Holy Spirit breaks them open to us.

Luther, however, found that the Scriptures he beat upon beat him back. He used to say, "The text is my adversary," meaning it stood against the sinfulness within him, confronting the evil that remained within his heart. Similarly, one pastor has referred to Romans 9 as a tiger who devoured him—that it declared a truth he could not escape though he wanted to. Reading and studying the Bible is like a great boxing match where we beat on the text with our minds, and the text beats back on the sin remaining in our hearts. But the gain is far greater than the struggle.

In Genesis 32 the sinful man Jacob (his name means "deceiver") wrestled with God. In the process he sustained a wound from which he limped the rest of his life, but he received a new name, a name that would characterize his new life: Israel (which means "struggles with God"). In a similar way, if we wrestle with God in the text of Scripture, He *will* wrestle us down—and we will gain a new name through which He will form a new character. Just as Jacob was never quite the same man again after that night, we will never be the same again either.

Putting it into practice

What I have urged you to seek is not the status quo. In fact, in an age with so few heroes I am always suspicious of the "normal" life. Let me just leave you with the encouragement that this can be done.

My freshman year in college, I made the decision that I wanted to read the Bible regularly, so I scheduled quiet times of reading and prayer into each day. I intentionally placed them during times when I wouldn't be sleepy, and where there wouldn't be a lot of social activities going on. For me, that was 11:00 a.m. to 12:00 noon. Almost every day I read a few chapters of the Bible, wrote a prayer in my journal related to what I had just read, and then prayed. I did that for my whole freshman year. I have never been even remotely the same man since.

I share this not to brag about what a godly person I am but to encourage you that it can be done. No one is born with knowledge of the Bible. We must become students of the Word, as we answer the call to a wrestling match with the Creator of the universe, for our good and for His glory.

6.

INTERACTING WITH THE WORLD

My wife, Heidi, became a Christian the summer before she went to college. This was a tad ironic given the fact that she was the president of her youth group her senior year. Nevertheless, during that summer, she attended a retreat, was presented with the gospel message, and was told that she needed to put her faith in Jesus in order to gain the gift of eternal life. She was extremely hesitant to do so. Why? Was it because she was a big partier and was mourning the loss of being in on that crazy scene? Nope. Was it because she had some serious intellectual difficulties with believing in Christ? Not really. Mostly, it was because she had heard the music that Christians listen to, and she thought: do I really have to listen to that junk? I mean, I guess I can if I have to, but is that part of the package?

Granted, since 1993, Christian music has come a long way, but still: I chuckle when I think about the obstacles that lay in non-believers' paths. It's often not Jesus himself. That part sounds kind of exciting. Rather, the obstacles lie in being required to live what is perceived as "the good Christian life." The question is: what does God require of them, and what do we as the Christian culture require of them? And how do we ensure that the former and not the latter is emphasized?

One of the finest caricatures of a Christian is the character Ned Flanders on *The Simpsons*. Ned is the classic cheesy Christian who only allows his children to play board games like "Clothe the Leper" and "Build a Mission." Ned punishes them by sending them to bed without a Bible story ("You knew I had a temper when you married me," he explains to his wife, Maude).

Maude goes away on a retreat in order to learn how to be more judgmental, and the extent of their marital problems lie in Ned's frustration with her propensity to "underline passages in my Bible when she can't find hers." While Ned is sometimes the hero of storylines and has a ripped upper body (as revealed when he portrays Stanley in the musical version of *A Streetcar Named Desire*), let's face it: the man is a boob. Homer is the real hero, and Ned is the butt of jokes. One can only assume that a good many people perceive Christians like this.

Singer/songwriter Justin McRoberts sells a great T-shirt at his concerts. It's green with simple yellow lettering on the front: "They'll know we are Christians by our T-shirts." I would add bumper stickers and jewelry to that list as well. His point is a great one: we as Christians have decided that the easiest way to communicate God's very profound and revolutionary message to the watching world is by wearing T-shirts that say "God's Gym" or "His Pain, Your Gain," or by putting bumper stickers on our cars that say "In Case of Rapture, This Car Will Be Unmanned."

Years ago, I was at a park and was dumbfounded to see a grade school boy wearing a shirt that said the name of his church, above which was a giant "One Way" sign, with the arrow pointing up. That's a way to bring in the newcomers, I thought. Look Phyllis, a church that thinks they have the only true way! I bet those are nice, open-minded people! Excuse me, sonny, when are your church's services?

Now don't get me wrong. I agree that the New Testament teaches that Jesus is the only way to the Father (John 14:6) and that salvation is found in no other name (Acts 4:12). This is foundational Christian belief. But did it ever occur to the church that this shirt might appear at all offensive to someone? That it might be a stumbling block to someone's coming to faith? I mean, what's the point of making a shirt like this? Why not just go all the way, and say: "If you can read this shirt, and you don't know Jesus, you're heading straight to hell! But I'm not! Suckah!!"

It occurred to me that this church had spent very little time contemplating how others might perceive them due to the message on their shirts. Either that, or they simply didn't care what a nonbeliever might think. To me, that is antithetical to Jesus's basic message, and to God's heart for the lost. Jesus said that he came to seek and to save that which was lost. He came for the sick, not the healthy. He tells the story in Luke 15 of the father longing for his children to come home. We have to be aware of how others might perceive us, and not put any more obstacles than already exist in the way of an unbeliever who might want to investigate Christianity.

The Christian ghetto

Many Christians live inside their Christian ghettos. They hunker down inside their isolated cities, and shoot anyone who tries to climb over the walls. It's Christian music, Christian videos, Christian friends from Christian families, Christian theme parks on their Christian vacations: all Christian, all the time! I read a letter in a Christian magazine where someone responded to the issue of sending a child to a public school. "There is no room for compromise," he wrote. "Six or seven hours a day of the world and its ways? No, no, no!" I'm not opposed to Christian education, but I wonder if he had ever thought about a Christian's role in positively influencing "the world and its ways."

Jesus tells us in Matthew 5 that our job is to be salt and light. Salt is useless when it stays in the shaker, and as Jesus pointed out, it would be downright silly to light a candle, then put a bowl on top of it. Our job is to be a part of the culture, to influence it for good from the inside. Of course, we have to do so in a way that doesn't allow the world's priorities to become ours, but that is not an impossible task, with the Lord's help.

The alternative, to separate ourselves from the culture and create a "Christian" subculture, is not something I find in the Bible. Some might quote 2 Corinthians 6:17, which urges believers to "come out from them and be separate." But this is in the context of being "yoked together" with unbelievers, which means that believers should not be identified with nonbelievers by joining in with their pagan actions. It is a call to holy living, not a command to retreat from the sinful masses.

When it's necessary

Sometimes it is important for Christians to separate themselves from unhealthy lifestyles and situations for a time, in order to gain perspective and free themselves from patterns of sin. And the power of the Christian community is so important in this situation. But the goal of this time away should be to gain healing in order to return and be part of impacting the world for good.

There are also times when it might be important for an individual to take a personal stand for Christ. I remember that when I was a freshman at DePaul my faith was just taking off, and wearing a rather large cross around my neck was an important step for me in terms of identifying myself with Christ.

For others of you heading to college wondering if you'll follow through on your commitment to Jesus, wearing some kind of outward sign representative of your faith like a bracelet or necklace may help you get connected with other Christians. And it may be a faith-building activity to make such a stand in front of your peers. But we do need to exercise wisdom, and at least keep in mind how others are perceiving us and, by extension, Christ and the church.

It'll be messy

You also have to be very careful that during your time in college, you don't escape into an "us versus them" mentality. In one episode of *The Simpsons*, Bart and Lisa go to Reverend Lovejoy to ask for the phone number of the rabbi in town. The Reverend first asks them to reconsider their decision to convert. When he learns that they aren't planning to do that, he brightens up and says: "No problem, let me just get his phone number out of my non-Christian Rolodex."

What a keen commentary on how we as Christians divide up our lives. We have our Christian friends, and our non-Christian friends. We even have different names for when we hang out with them: one is Fellowship, and the other is Outreach. And how about when the groups comingle? Oh, the terror! You hope that your outspoken Christian friends don't talk too much about God, or start praying out loud right in front of everyone, and you hope that your really salty non-Christian friends don't drop too many f-bombs during the conversation. It's a mess, isn't it?

I'm not saying that I have the answer, but I think it's just OK to embrace the messiness for what it is: the world we live in this side of glory.

Expect lots of sin

I was watching a professional sports game with some friends a while back, and when the conversation shifted to one of the players, many of us expressed our admiration for him. One friend (a Christian) said: "I can't stand him; he cheated on his wife." I've heard similar comments about other prominent figures. "I can't watch him in a movie," another friend says, "because of how he was caught with another woman." My response is: *of course* they did. *Of course* people who aren't followers of Christ sleep around and lie and cheat and steal. Heck, plenty of Christ-followers do those things, too. But the point is: we should *expect* people who are far from God to act as though they're far from God.

I honestly don't know how people stay married if they don't know Jesus. I'm shocked when I hear of marriages that *do* work when the couples aren't committed Christians. Why? Because sin is so powerful and so destructive! I don't doubt that I would be divorced by now if I weren't a Christ-follower. We have to expect non-Christians to act accordingly, and shouldn't simply seek to clean up their lives. Our goal is not behavior modification, as though we're their therapists seeking merely to help them "make healthy decisions." Our goal is to help sinners become reconciled with their Heavenly Father, and to then let the Holy Spirit transform them from the inside out.

The Three Bs

The best way to do that for someone outside the church is to let them know that there's a place for them in the church. Community is one of the most powerful incentives we can offer a non-Christian. Before we seek to help someone understand our message, they have to know that they can be a part of the game. They can play, too. A little wordplay that I borrowed and adjusted slightly from Mike Pilavachi at Soul Survivor in Watford, England, is as follows: the process that some churches expect outsiders to follow is "Believe, Behave, Belong." First, they need to believe what we're teaching, then they're certainly going to have to clean up their act and behave differently, then we'll meet in one of our committees to discuss whether we'll let them in.

The better way is "Belong, Believe, Become." First of all, whether they share our beliefs or not, they have a place here. There's always room for them. Then, as they feel welcomed, they will have the proper context and perhaps the desire to want to know what it is that we believe. And finally, the behavior isn't ever the point. Instead, it's about *becoming* all that God wants us to be in Christ.

Do we truly believe in the concept of grace or not? Do we believe that while we were still sinners, Christ died for us? Can we show those far from God that it's not about *their* righteousness, but about Christ's righteousness? Do we trust in God's kindness to lead sinners to repentance (Rom. 2) or do we think He needs our man-made regulations to help Him?

Our goal as Christians should be to infiltrate the culture in order to impact it for good. In the passage from Matthew 5 where Jesus is talking about our role as salt and light, He says the following: "In the same way, let your light shine before men, that they may see your good deeds and praise your Father in heaven." Jesus is talking specifically about our good deeds. He doesn't even mention here that we need to "share our faith" or "convert" anyone; He is simply encouraging His followers to live holy, transparent lives, and stating that the deeds displayed by those lives will be what makes the impact.

Francis of Assisi's oft-quoted line is helpful: "Preach the gospel. Use words if necessary." Now, this doesn't relieve us of our need to be ready to "give an answer to everyone who asks [us] to give a reason for the hope that [we] have" (1 Pet. 3:15). We should all be prepared to articulate a clear explanation of what it means to follow Jesus, but that explanation will be unwelcome or hollow if our lives haven't communicated that message first.

A final word on music

Since I opened the chapter with a reference to Christian music, I'd like to take just a moment and further address the issue. Very likely, your view on Christian music will be defined by your parents' views, the friends you hang out with, and the part of the country you grew up in. In some circles, being a Christian means that you must only listen to Christian music. In others, Christian music is largely ignored. The bottom line is this: listening to Christian music doesn't earn you brownie points with God.

For some of you, this is the only reason you listen to Christian music: so you can be a completely "good Christian." But from my standpoint, the question shouldn't be: is the music Christian? The question is: how does the music affect you?

It's largely a heart issue. If listening to secular music depresses you, or encourages you to set your heart on things that distract you from God, then by all means, don't listen to it! On the other hand, if you are listening to Christian music not because you like it but because you're "supposed to," don't bother! Music should encourage us, stir us up, and cause us to worship God. But don't think that secular music can't do that just as easily as Christian music. When a musician or a songwriter creates something beautiful, that makes me thank God, whether the artist is a Christian or not. Thus, some Sigur Ros or Coldplay songs can cause me to worship as much as (though perhaps in a different way than) a Hillsong or David Crowder tune (and I enjoy them all!). And what's more, if all we're listening to is Christian music, we take another step closer to the heart of the Christian ghetto, and we further alienate ourselves from the rest of the world.

Furthermore, our young Christian musicians (and other Christian artists, for that matter) need to be encouraged to pursue excellence in their craft, and to make strides on the secular scene, as artists like Jars of Clay and Switchfoot have been able to do. These bands have become popular because they're good, not because they're Christians. And consequently, they have been able to have an impact with their music far beyond what they would have had in just the Christian realm.

There's a place for Christian music, as long as it's not the only place in town.

REBECCA'S STORY

When it came to that time senior year when I was faced with making a college decision, I had no idea what I wanted or where to even start in the application process. I didn't track a favorite college sport, I wasn't raised with affiliation to a family school, and I wasn't even passionate about a particular area of study. Like most high schoolers, I had gone on visits to schools while in the process of the college search, but left without the "magical feeling of belonging." My head spiraled with lists of pros and cons and endless wondering about where I could see myself in those next four years. When it came down to it, the most important question I had to think about was: which college was going to help me be the person I wanted to *become*? After wrestling with this question, it was clear that a particular school would foster the community I longed for and the opportunities for involvement in the local surroundings that would help develop who I wanted to be. Even though my decision was finally made, I was unaware of the journey that lay ahead in breaking down my expectations of what I thought college "should be" and giving myself time and space to create my own unique journey. I arrived at school brimming with excitement for a new community, and I immediately immersed myself in every social situation, convinced that this would lead me to best friends. Yet most nights I found that being surrounded by people all day did not forge deep friendships, but instead left me lonely and drained. If I wanted friendships that were deep and intimate, I had to build a foundation on something bigger than school activities.

When I finally chose a church to commit to and a small group to invest in, it was clear that I was meant to do life in the context of Christ-centered community, and these people became my family. The girls in my small group were soon my roommates for the three following years, and the girls who know me better than anyone ever could. Although I could have easily been too tired or busy for church during college, I disciplined myself to make this investment a priority because I knew it was where growth would happen and lives would be changed. For me, college was all about community, and there's no better time and place to make lifelong community happen. The more years I live post-college, the more real it becomes to see friends scatter to new places and start new lives. I am forever thankful that I spent my college years living life alongside the people that challenged me to be the best version of myself, encouraged growth and intimacy with God, and loved me no matter what. Investing eternally in people's lives is what makes college the worthwhile experience that impacts you years after college is over. There's no other way I would've chosen to live those four years, and I continue to be renewed and refined by the friendships forged during that time.

EDITING YOUR LIFE

It is true that there is much free time in college. This is not always the case, but most will find this to be so. I remember my first fall at Oswego. I lived in a dorm overlooking a large field where each day there was a gathering of people to play sports. My roommates and I played football, soccer, ultimate Frisbee, broomball, basketball, and tennis. Many nights we stayed up playing video games like *Goldeneye* or the latest EA Sports creation, and on certain nights we piled into the ninth-floor lounge to watch *Friends* (in its first season) and the *X-files.* Do students today even know these shows? Never mind. The point is: I had a lot of free time in college, and I fully enjoyed it.

I know this is not necessarily true of all college students. A bright education major with good study habits at a state school like mine has a different amount of free time than a physics major at MIT. Further, there is a big difference between the college experience of a person taking nineteen hours of coursework while working on the side, and mine where my mommy and daddy paid for everything. Regardless of what category you find yourself in, it is always a good idea to take a step back and consider how best to use your time.

The Crazy Child and the Editor

Within each of us there is a creative person who is game for almost anything. This is what my good friend David calls the

"Crazy Child." The freedom of college life is intoxicating, and we want to drink it in for all it's worth; you know, *carpe diem* and all that. After the minute-managed high school life many lead, going to class fifteen hours a week seems nice, and we have all kinds of time for new and exciting experiences. That's good. Try some of them. But after a while you will begin to see that the Crazy Child in you is wasteful. He sleeps too much, watches too much TV, enjoys YouTube more than studying, doesn't read the Bible unless he feels like it, and he usually falls asleep in prayer. Bad Crazy Child.

That's when you need the voice of maturity called "the Editor." She is here to make sure your fun life isn't a waste. She is the one saying, "Hey, all this fun stuff is good, but what are you accomplishing? Who are you striving to become? How is God calling you to live?" Usually the Editor is a group of voices saying roughly the same thing. Sometimes the voice of the Editor comes from your parents, sometimes from Scripture or from the pulpit, sometimes directly from your conscience—but no matter how she speaks to you, she is there, so listen.

The voice of the Holy Spirit can sound like both the Editor and the Crazy Child. The Holy Spirit calls you to a more disciplined and productive existence, but he is also an adventurous and bold spirit, and wants you to experience life in its fullness. God wants you to live with passion *and* with discipline, so you must learn to hear the voice of God in both the Crazy Child *and* the Editor.

A Christian view of time use

This leads to an important question. Is there a Christian understanding of time use that should be applied to the college years? This is important for a couple of reasons.

First, you need to know and keep reminding yourself that God relates to *everything* through Christ. As Abraham Kuyper has said, "There is not a square inch in the whole domain of our human existence over which Christ, who is sovereign over *all*, does not cry: 'Mine!' " This is true even of your time.

Second, you are still technically in adolescence. You are still forming important habits, and these habits will follow you the rest of your adult life. Your habits concerning time are exceedingly important since time is your greatest commodity. Ben Franklin used to say, "Time *is* life."

So what priorities does God put before us to be applied in our use of time? Ephesians 5:15–18 says:

Therefore watch how you live, not as unwise but as wise, making the most of your time, since the days are evil. So then do not be foolish, but understand the will of the Lord. And do not get drunk with wine, for that is dissipation, but be filled with the Spirit.

What is Paul getting at? There are at least two things we can put our fingers on. First, our use of time defines our lifestyle and determines whether our lives are wise or foolish. Do you see the relationship between "watch how you live" and "making the most of your time"? Making the most of our time is the way Paul calls us to watch how we live. He makes his point negatively, that we should avoid "dissipation" and then positively, that we should use our time to be filled with the Holy Spirit. We do this for two reasons.

First, because the days are evil, and second because it is the "Lord's will." This specific passage is worthy of further meditation, but it is only the tip of an iceberg of truth that applies to our use of time. Once we realize that our life is made up of consecutive minutes and seconds, it is hard not to understand that the spiritual success or failure of our life is inseparably bound up in how we use our time. Worship takes time. Reading takes time. Prayer takes time. In fact, every spiritual discipline God uses to fill us with his Spirit, giving us spiritual power over sin and spiritual potency in ministry, takes time.

The heart of the matter

Quote all the verses you want about God's will for us to use our time well, but the question still remains: why? Why is it God's will that we exercise wisdom and not waste excessive amounts of time in mindless recreation and empty amusement? We need the reason not just because we're being "difficult," but to get the motivation we need to tell our flesh who's boss. We need to understand the root of the matter in order to have the practical self-discipline to shut off the X-Box, get out of bed, turn off the TV, open our Bibles, get some exercise, and spend time in prayer. It isn't easy to turn away from the amusement of the moment to invest in the possibilities of the future.

The heart of the matter here is *mission.* God is doing something. He is saving humanity from death, hell, sin, and itself. When you became a follower of Jesus, no matter what you thought you were doing, you were also joining God's mission on Earth. You were not just liberated from sin, wrath, and judgment. You did not just start a relationship with God so you could call Him up if you had some pressing need. The Gospel of Christ is not nearly so human-centered as that. God did not become *yours* so much as you gained the privilege of becoming *His*. You became one of His instruments to save a dying world. That's why we have to make the most of our time: we are God's servants and soldiers in His great campaign to save humanity.

This is why Paul, a son of God, called himself a *"bondservant* of Jesus Christ" in Romans 1:1 and elsewhere. It is the same reason he told Timothy to "endure suffering like a good *soldier* of Christ Jesus" (2 Tim. 2:3). They understood, as we must, that though they were heirs of all the amazing promises of Jesus Christ (Gal. 3:29), they were also His unconditional servants in the mission He left for them to complete. It is for this mission that Paul said we "labor and strive" (1 Tim. 4:10, Col. 1:29) and for which he exhorted Timothy to "training" (1 Tim. 4:7).

This is why Paul said, "the days are evil." It is not the time itself that is morally corrupt. It is that this temporal, sin-saturated world is passing away. Our short lives will soon be over, and the window of opportunity to harness our lives for something that will impact the destiny of history is fleeting. Today is not simply another day of meager import, but it is of infinite consequence.

Since each day has the potential to impact eternity, each day is immensely meaningful and strategic; Christ has called us to use our time, intellect, and finances with this in mind. If you allow the priorities of Christ to really shape your own agenda, you simply will not be tempted to waste excesses of time.

Avoiding neurosis

Once we realize that this whole time thing is about understanding and participating in God's mission, we lose the weak and destructive conception that God is against fun and recreation. He is not, given that it has its proper place. Good soldiers have fun. Useful servants learn when to work hard to please the master and when it is time to party. Athletes know when it is time to eat, drink, and laugh, and when it is time for intense training and competition. Jesus Himself claimed His yoke was easy and His burden light; He knew when it was time to be intensely about His Father's work and when it was time to rest and relax. You must as well, and this balance cannot be achieved until you think hard about it.

It is important to understand that you are not God's accountant, making sure every second is totally accounted for in a neurotic and slavish way. God is not a hard taskmaster, driving us to the brink of exhaustion for no purpose. Instead, you are his steward or servant (see Matt. 25:14–30), given authority over certain assets of the Master (your life, skills, possessions, and finances) in order to bring him profit in his mission.

God is seeking to coach you in order for you to be more fruitful in your life's mission: fulfilling His. We each have to get away from the idea of being our own neurotic taskmaster and seek to live a disciplined, spiritually profitable life.

The point of this chapter is simple: God cares how you spend your time. We should never lose sight of that. College often has a lot of unstructured time. Enjoy yourself. Play sports, hang out, and stay up all night playing video games at least once. But it is also a great opportunity for you to invest a strategic season of your life in spiritual growth, intellectual development, and direct ministry. Read some good books, pray, read your Bible, and be involved in ministry. Take time to establish good spiritual fundamentals now, and you will reap great benefits the rest of your life.

There is pleasure in amusement and recreation. This is a good and memorable time. Yet do not forget that there is a deeper joy in the things of Christ. There is nothing so inspiring as seeing the beauty of Jesus Christ a bit more clearly in study and prayer, or so great as the thrill of leading someone to discover Christ in their life and seeing them enjoying a new kind of life as a result. Deeper joys are always won through discipline, time, and pain, and they are worth ten thousand mediocre worldly thrills. There is a triumphant joy that can only be found on the battlefield. God has always intended that we find our deepest joy in the struggles of life, not in our escapes from them.

8.
FINDING
A CHURCH HOME

I know, I know. You'll never find another youth group like yours. You'll never find a church where you'll fit in. Four years is such a short amount of time. Why would I get plugged into a place that I know I'll be leaving soon? These are all wonderful excuses, really. We're all proud of you. But they are not persuasive.

The reality is this: your faith will face enormous opposition in college, from professors, fellow students, and even from your own heart, as you begin to ask harder and deeper questions than you've ever asked. Couple that with an atmosphere where sin is not just prevalent or encouraged, but expected, and you have a recipe for a real faith crisis. Do not be unaware of the severity of these challenges. What are the primary weapons to fight these? As Nic mentioned earlier, one is personal (your own hidden life with God) and one is communal, your involvement in a local ministry. Unless you are connected to a local ministry, your faith is likely to wither and die.

For some, it comes down to a question of independence. Sometimes, a student will get to the place where he thinks he doesn't need anyone else, as long as he has Jesus. Either that, or no church is ever good enough for her. The writer of the book of Hebrews has this advice: "Let us not give up meeting together, as some are in the habit of doing, but let us encourage one another—and all the more as you see the Day approaching" (10:25). This advice is given in the context of a call to draw near to God, to receive what we need from

Him, and to not turn from the strength of our convictions. Clearly, this cannot happen on our own. There is no such thing as a Lone-Ranger Christian. The Bible never gives any hint that "just you and Jesus" can work things out, unless you're talking about you and the body of Christ, which Scripture says is the church! The church is the presence of Jesus, and we simply will not be able to flourish as one of His followers without it.

My goal in this chapter is to convince you that if you take your faith seriously at all, and hope to make it a priority in college, you must find fellowship. Get a Game Plan for plugging in.

But why?

The two biggest excuses I hear for not plugging into a church are that it's just not the same, and that it's just four years. Let me address these.

No, of course you won't find anything *exactly* like your youth group. God is not in the business of doing the same thing over and over. He has *new* and *exciting* things ahead for you. The fact that you even have the opportunity to leave home and experience life in a different setting separates you from the vast majority of the world. Be thankful for the chance to be a part of new experiences, and be ready to embrace a new body of believers in your new setting.

And what can you really do in four years? Well, Jesus changed the world forever in three years, so I would think that four years is at least enough time to learn a thing or two from other Christians, don't you? So find fellowship. Don't wait a few weeks so you can get your bearings, don't wait till you find out whether you're a Tri-Delt or a Kappa, don't wait till you get "settled in." Do it first. And do it on two fronts.

On campus: A parachurch group

If you're attending a secular university, chances are there is a Christian group (called a parachurch group, meaning "alongside the church") of some kind already on campus. The biggest and most recognized are InterVarsity Christian Fellowship, Cru, and Navigators. However, at many schools, they have chosen more ambiguous names such as The Well, or have incorporated the school's name in their title (for instance, Miami Christian Fellowship at Miami University in Ohio is actually an InterVarsity chapter). On most campuses there are also denominational groups such as a Catholic Student Center, an Episcopal/Anglican Student Center, an Eastern Orthodox Student Fellowship, a Presbyterian Student Fellowship—you get the idea.

There are a few names you should avoid. University Bible Fellowship (UBF) and the International Church of Christ (ICOC, sometimes called the Boston movement) are unhealthy fellowships that center mostly around controlling you, and they often prey on college students. Politely decline invitations to their meetings. If you're curious about whether a church is a cult or not, a Google search can certainly help you out.

If you happen to be at a campus where there are truly no organized Christian groups, then start praying about how God might use you to start one during your four years there. Both Nic and I were involved in planting campus groups during college, and the process was a thrilling one for both of us. Don't underestimate what God can do through you during your time there. There are often InterVarsity and Cru chapters nearby, and you can contact existing staff for help in getting started.

I must warn you (this is very important, pay attention to this): it is highly unlikely that you will immediately (or perhaps ever) find the same kind of community that you came out of in high school. In fact, it's more likely that you will find yourself connecting first with students outside of the Christian fellowship. It's sort of like the difference between your friends and your family.

You get to pick your friends, but not your family. In some cases, your family will also be your friends, but not always. So don't be surprised when you don't quickly connect with the Christians on your campus. You may find yourself saying things like: I would never be friends with these people if they weren't Christians. Or: all the Christians on campus are nerds. Or: I'm a nerd, and all these Christians are too cool for their own good. That's OK! You don't *have* to be great friends with any of them. Just be willing to remain committed to them regardless, and let your shared commitment to Jesus be your bond. But don't let your lack of connection drive you away from pursuing Christian fellowship. The body of Christ is intended to be a diverse body that accepts all types. Some you will like and some you won't. But God loves them all.

Off campus: A local church

This will often be particularly challenging to those of you without cars. But you will likely meet upperclassmen with cars who attend church (or who know their way around public transportation, as was the case my freshman year). The easiest way to find a church is to ask the older classes: where do people go to church? Try a few of them, and if they aren't what you're looking for, check the yellow pages. For some of you, this will feel like overkill. If you are connecting and getting spiritually fed by your campus ministry, then for some of you, that group might serve as your church. However, I feel strongly that there is tremendous value in being connected to an intergenerational body of believers while you are in college, and this can only happen in a local church. I read recently that high school students who connected only with a youth group and not with a church are less likely to attend church after college than those students who attended church but not a youth group. Maintaining a pattern of regular Sunday morning (or evening) church attendance is an important habit to either start or continue.

When you're visiting churches, pay attention to several things. First of all, ask for their statement of faith. It's always a good thing to give that a quick once-over just to make sure there's nothing odd there. Some of the looniest cults can look pretty normal at first glance. If you have questions about any of their statements, follow up with someone.

Second, check to see if they acknowledge the presence of college students at all. They may not have a college ministry, but that's OK; you may not need that. The question is: do they have any sense of being welcoming to college students? Are there opportunities for you to be involved in the church beyond just Sunday morning attendance? And obviously, observe the service itself and see if it's a place where you can be challenged, encouraged, and fed spiritually.

The last thing to keep your eyes open for is the opportunity to be mentored. For me and for many of my friends, it was the mentors we found in our churches while in college that transformed our lives. It was getting the opportunity to be around Christian couples and their families that taught me what it meant to be a godly husband and father. Because many college fellowship staff workers are recent college grads, they won't be able to meet this need. Most churches don't have a formal system set up to make this happen, but plugging into a ministry in the church can sometimes lead to a natural mentoring relationship with a church leader, whether they are on staff or not. Take advantage of this opportunity if you can!

Having a church is also important because it gives you a place to start giving financially. Now obviously, while you're in college no church is going to get rich off of your giving, but you need to start setting a pattern of regular giving when you're young and poor, so that when you're older and less poor, it won't even be an issue.

In most cases, you should have been able to visit enough churches by Thanksgiving of your freshman year to have found a church to call home.

A final note on worship styles

I'm a music snob when it comes to church music. I'll freely admit that. What that means is that I can be quite particular about the worship style that I'm partial to, and about those that I do not favor. On the plus side, this has made me a good worship leader, and has helped others value what is important in a worship time: creating a context whereby people can have an experience with God, focusing on Him and not on the people up front. But I also realize that I may have made it difficult for students in my youth group to participate in churches that don't "do worship" like they're used to.

The reality is that you may not find a church or fellowship with what you or I would call "a good worship experience." You have two alternatives at this point. You can either shake your head and say: "This music is terrible. I'm out of here." Or you can say: "The worship atmosphere in this group isn't what I'm used to, and it isn't what I would choose. But church is bigger than just one thing. So are there enough other things going on at this church that would make it worth connecting with?"

There will be times in your life when you will have to sacrifice what your preference would be for what God has called you to. There is no perfect church. Most churches will be better at one thing or another: one church has really good music, another has great teaching, and still another will exude a warmth that just makes you want to be there with the people.

In our consumer culture, our tendency is to want to take our business elsewhere, always looking for the better deal, and so on. If you are living a life of worship to God, you should be able to worship God at church even if you don't prefer the songs they're singing that week. Bottom line: find fellowship or face the frustration of a frail faith!

HEATHER'S STORY

I do not like change. When I was a senior in high school I spent most of my time hating the idea of leaving the close group of friends I had created in my youth group. When I finally got excited about the Christian university I was attending, it was partially because two of my best friends were going to the same school. I looked forward to continuing my Christian life and community in an explicitly Christian environment. These rather mild expectations were quickly disappointed. As a shy and generally uncomfortable eighteen-year-old, the upheaval of a totally new way of life in a mob of strangers would have been a challenge for me no matter where I went. But moving from a public high school to a Christian university was a shock that I was utterly unprepared for. I soon learned that the countercultural attitude my faith had taken at home did not make sense in my new context.

I could no longer define myself by the friends I had or the church I went to; the identity I had formed in high school was stripped of its external supports. It was unnerving. Thrown into a Christian culture I had never been exposed to, I struggled to understand my faith in a new way and to find somewhere I fit in. Meanwhile, the friends I came to college with became involved in a large church whose style of worship and teaching made me extremely uncomfortable. I didn't fit in the home they were finding, I couldn't find my own home, and almost by default my self-understanding became negative.

I increasingly defined who I was by who I wasn't, and cynicism toward certain churches, types of Christians, and denominations took the place of my high school rejection of worldliness. The confusion and loneliness of my freshman year gave way to an embittered satisfaction in the fact that I did not fit in. I stopped looking for a church home and even went so far as to tell my old youth ministers (Syler and Nic) that *everyone* should take at least a year off of church in their lives. I became friends with people who seemed more genuine in their faith to me merely because they drank, smoked, smelled bad, and didn't look like the glossy image of popular Christianity I had come to reject. But the longer I understood myself only by declaring what I wasn't, the less there seemed to be of what I actually was. By my junior year I was longing for a solid path not built on rejection.

My courses in philosophy and literature were part of what brought me to this point. The delight in God's truth I had experienced in my high school church, and was looking for in all of the churches I visited in college, I found in a place where I was not used to looking: the classroom. Faith, learning, and the pursuit of wisdom had only ever been combined for me in an exclusively religious setting. I had always thought and read in high school, but then I spent more time on the C.S. Lewis books church leaders recommended to me than I did on my schoolwork. The more time I spent with thinkers and writers like St. Augustine, St. Thomas Aquinas, Dante, the Inklings, and Flannery O'Connor, the more my thoughtlife was guided and deepened by faithful professors, the more my questions and (often petty) discontents were contextualized and judged by comparison.

The life of faith was no longer a choice between the cheap cultural Christianity that costs its members so little on one hand and a rebellion in favor of edgy-looking faith so focused on not being hypocritical that it centered on social justice more than God on the other. My conception of the church changed from a faulty institution I could choose to accept or reject, to the living body of Christ on earth that I could not avoid without also turning from the God I supposedly followed. Exhausted, no longer wanting to be defined by what I was not, I became a member of the liturgical church that many of my professors attended and I actively pursued a "positive definition."

Ultimately, this search for what I call a positive definition led me to the rich, living body of Scripture, tradition, liturgy, and sacrament that refuses negative definition. In the positive structure of the Catholic Church, I have found a home that does not reject but incorporates my evangelical high school experience, university rebellion, and current ecumenical community. Looking at the odd sweeps of the path I took to get here, I am reminded of the first time I consciously encountered the truth of God in an academic setting. I vividly remember sitting in my Intro to Philosophy class on St. Augustine's *Confessions* and recognizing for the first time what it might mean that we are made for God and won't work apart from Him. "Our hearts are restless until they rest in You." Through the fairly continual frustration and dissatisfaction I experienced in college I am grateful for one thing above all else: my dissatisfaction. Not with others, but with the state of my own faith. As Flannery O'Connor wrote to a struggling freshman in college, "If you want your faith, you have to work for it. It is a gift, but for very few is it a gift given without any demand for equal time devoted to its cultivation."

9.

YOUR FAITH
AND YOUR MAJOR

The nature of the university education beast is that sooner or later you must pick both a field of study and a major within that field. That is not always true of those who manage to take a "liberal arts" major, but we might note that these folks usually are forced to go on to graduate school and have the same dilemma thrust upon them at that point. Either way, we all choose a major, or at least an occupation. We all ultimately choose an academic field to enter, and at least for a time, sustain ourselves and make our personal contribution within that field.

I remember the first time I selected a major on a college application. I was in my guidance counselor's office and she insisted that I not mark the "undeclared" box since it wasn't fashionable at that time to not know "what you want to do with your life." So in order to humor her and myself, I marked three different majors on three different applications: business, psychology, and history.

Although many students are more certain by that point about what field they will pursue in college, their decision is often not related in their minds distinctly to their faith. It's true that it usually is related in the sense that they have decided that careers in lap dancing and organized crime assassination are probably not going to work out morally with their decision to be a Christ follower, but many students barely get further than this. The burden of this chapter is to explain mainly the importance, but also the tactics, of what has been called "Christian integration," the organization of all of life, including your field, into a coherent relevant personal theology.

Difficulty and Importance

Christian integration is not easy, but it is extremely important. Now I understand it's difficult to sense the pleasure of God while pulling an organic chemistry all-nighter; I have personally struggled with understanding how my faith related to my business major. But, the failure to think through what it means to be a Christ follower in your particular field has certain important consequences.

First, we have to think about the proposition of work as a whole. Most of us will spend between 35 and 65 hours working each week for most of our adult lives. Therefore, *your occupation will almost certainly occupy the best hours of most of the days during the best years of your life.* If you fail to think about work now, this may well become more of a sentence than a privilege.

Second, your work is potentially one of your biggest contributions to your community and world. Some jobs take away from community and society, but others lead the way in the distribution of mercy, the administration of justice, the investigation of God's glorious cosmos and the creation of honest work for others. Pastors are not the only ones who are doing God's work in the world. Christians have amazing opportunities to influence the world for good as professors, lawyers, teachers, engineers, mothers, doctors, nurses, social workers, investors, architects, law enforcement officers, builders, sanitation workers, and so on. Consider that your work will not just be a way of making a living, but will provide a means and a place in which to glorify God.

This life integration is undoubtedly easier for some than for others. I have worked both as a high school teacher in a public high school and as a seating host in a large restaurant. I can clearly say that it was easier to understand how teaching humanities to youth seemed to relate to my faith more directly than my telling people, "Here are your menus. You can take the second booth on the left."

However, I can also say with integrity that it was my faith that motivated me to do my repetitive and stressful host job with excellence and joy. The fact that I was able to see handing out oil-stained menus as God's will for me at that moment gave meaning to an otherwise meaningless situation and motivated me to do it with excellence as an offering to my loving God. That attitude, which came from a theological conviction, kept me both sane and happy in a very stressful low-paying job and opened up numerous platforms for me to share Christ with people all around me.

Good theologian, bad theologian

The obvious point of the above examples is to motivate you to start thinking theologically about the work component of your life now. Thinking theologically about your career, however, is just a single application of one of my biggest ministry mantras: everyone is a theologian; the only question is, "Are you a good theologian or a bad one?" The task of Christian integration mentioned above is simply the task of thinking theologically about all of life and then actually applying that theology to your life in particular. John Piper has rightly said, "[Theology] is about how God relates to *everything in the universe,* or how *everything in the universe* relates to God."[11] Part of being a Christian is to figure out what that relationship is and putting it into practice. If you don't accept the fact that you are a theologian in the most general sense, you will not feel responsible to examine every area of your life and ask, "How does this relate to God, and how does that affect that way I interact with it?"

---

11. John Piper, "The Preacher's Personal Pursuit of God" (lecture, Trinity Evangelical Divinity School, Deerfield, IL, October 2000.)

There are a couple of negative consequences of a lack of theological integration (especially in the area of work) that come from what might be called "compartmentalization." Compartmentalization happens when we either put our idea of God in a box in our minds, or put something in a private mental box by naively thinking, "God doesn't really relate to this."

Trying to put God in little boxes or "compartments" is both unbiblical and impractical. Sometimes we do this to try to hide from God because we don't want to obey Him in a particular area, but other times we just don't understand that God has something to say about every area of our lives, including the four areas we naturally want Him to talk to us about least: how we spend our money, how we indulge in romance, how we spend our leisure, and what we'll do for a career.

Although it is our natural, sinful tendency to hide these areas from God, He wants them most of all for two reasons. Since these four areas make up the majority of your time and assets, it is with them that both your *personal happiness* and *kingdom usefulness* are at stake.

First, your personal happiness is at stake because not integrating God's truth into an area of your life will eventually gut that area of its intended meaning, and subsequently, its joy. At first, when we feel that God doesn't relate to a particular area of our lives, we feel a freedom that seems liberating, but in the long run the areas where we think God is unrelated are found to have little meaning, and we begin to see our motivation leaking away in the monotonous repetition of our tasks. However, if we understand that God does relate to our work, and that the work itself, how we do it, and the income it provides are all important to Him, doing our work with meaning and excellence comes much more naturally.

The second reason God wants all of these four strategic areas for Himself is that he wants your life to be useful and full of excellence. If we wrongly think our work is meaningless, or just a means of making a living, we often don't think about the importance of usefulness and excellence in our work lives.

My wife and I both love the movie *Return to Me,* in which Carroll O'Connor plays Marty, a devout Irish Catholic restaurant owner in Chicago. One evening Grace, his granddaughter, asks him if he needs help as he finishes arranging chairs and closing up the restaurant. His response is, "No, no dear, I'm blessed with work." His understanding that it was a privilege to do something useful (even arranging chairs), and to have the opportunity to do it well made his work a blessing. His character's life was both useful and excellent.

Theologically we need to observe that work is a blessing, and, therefore, so is our career and academic field. Genesis 2:15, which comes before the curse of the fall, says, "The LORD God took the man and put him in the Garden of Eden *to work it and take care of it.*" God made humans with the intention that they would work, and that their work would be meaningful and fulfilling.

Lastly, because God has given our lives, and therefore our work, meaning and usefulness, He wants us to strive for excellence. Scripture says we are to do everything we do "for the glory of God" and "in the name of the Lord Jesus" (1 Cor. 10:31, Col. 3:17).

Nothing done for God's glory and Christ's name can be done halfheartedly: neither our worship, nor our work. Everything we do is for the glory of God and the honor of the name of Christ: how we spend our money, how we enjoy romance, what we do with our leisure, and certainly what we do for our career. This is true whether we dig ditches or preach sermons, whether we have five different careers or work in the same place our entire life. We have to constantly and in every situation strive not to just glorify God at work, but through our work.

Strategies for integrated career and major selection

Here are three ways to begin to think about how you can select a field that you will find meaningful and useful, and in which you can pursue excellence:

1. Consider your personality and abilities

First, recognize that we all come to this task a little differently. Scripture teaches in 1 Corinthians 12 and elsewhere that there is great diversity of gifts and abilities in the body of Christ. We all have both different kinds of gifts and different sized gifts from God, and that is exactly the way the Holy Spirit wants things. Because we all have these different aptitudes, we need to realistically look at ourselves and ask, "What has God made me to do?" His design of your personality and abilities are hints as to what He wants you to become. This is not a complete test in itself, but you should check your ambitions against it, and ask other people you trust if they think you are cut out for the field or career you are thinking about. Don't ask negative people who are just going to shoot you down; ask people who believe in you, know you, and yet are realistic. Take the hint from your limitations as well as your gifts.

2. Meditate on your passions and dreams

Second, take time to meditate on your passions and dreams. This is a *limited* strategy, but a very important one. It is limited in that if your passions have not been deeply renewed through your relationship with Christ, then your passions may not naturally lead you directly to God's will. However, if you are seeking to have your whole mind transformed by Christ (Rom. 12:1–2), then this can be a very helpful exercise. Take some time and ask yourself, "What do I really love? What do I find constantly interesting? Do I have a passion for people or tasks? What can I see myself doing and really enjoying? Do I love practical tasks, theoretical construction, or developing creative inspiration?" Ask yourself, or have someone ask you lots of questions like this.

Remember, you really don't know all the career opportunities out there, or what will exist when you graduate, so start by trying to understand what makes you tick and then apply it to a field. Don't narrow yourself down to your "one true passion," but try to understand your many different interests and how they function together to make you distinctly yourself. This "personal passion matrix" cannot independently select your career either, since most passions can be fulfilled in numerous ways, but if it is done well it will narrow the field of options considerably.

3. Think of work as a life and not merely a way to income

Last, think of your career as choosing a lifestyle, not just a means of making a living. You really can find both meaningful work and a way to make a living. Your years of work will be much of your legacy; so don't be financially practical to the exclusion of accomplishing something beautiful. Be practical, but don't be too practical. Don't make a life for yourself in which the only time you feel alive is when you are on vacation or at home. Spend your life well; you have but one. We *all* are called to the church, to serve her and support her work as a deep personal priority, but we are also called to be involved in medicine, science, economy, government, leisure, and many other amazing and wonderful graces that God gives the sinner as well as the righteous (Matt. 5:44–46).

Seven days of service

At the end of the day, you are not your career. Thank God. Work is not always fulfilling, and many people struggle with choosing a field, and then again with finding a job. It is also true that you will leave a ministry and family legacy besides your work. Yet, as I've said, our work is a central and exceedingly important area to allow God to say what he has to say to us.

We all stand at a crossroads of devotion. It is well and good that we serve God on the weekend, but God is asking for Monday through Friday as well. And if God is the God of our work, He is then the God of our field and major. What meaningful and useful work will you do with excellence for the glory of God? Have you thought about your choice of major this way? Will you?

10.

FACING TEMPTATION

This chapter is in homage to one of my heroes, C.S. Lewis. If you have never done so, read *The Screwtape Letters,* a series of pretend letters from a senior demon to his nephew about how to best steer a person away from God. What follows is my borrowing of his technique to address the ever-present struggle of the college student against temptation and sin. My hope is that it will encourage you to think, to read (or reread) *Screwtape,* and to take seriously your fight against the roaring lion that is prowling around, waiting for someone to devour (1 Pet. 5:8).

Subject: Re: He's off to College
Date: Fri, 16 Mar 2012 11:27:59 -0600
From: stank@wahoo.hell
To: tflanks@msoft.hell

My dear Tarflanks:

You're right. Our e-mail age brings with it all sorts of junk and forwards that you don't want to read. But look at it another way: I see it as a return to the art of letter writing. Once the telephone was invented, letter writing got relegated to the backseat in the newly "electronic" world.

Now, that same electricity has reintroduced us to letters! And so as your uncle, it will be an honor to be your "e-mentor" as your patient begins his journey into the university.

Your previous e-mail indicated some trepidation on your part that his Christian commitment has grown over the summer and will make your job much more difficult. Nonsense. There couldn't have been a better time for him to head off to college! If you thought high school presented a world of opportunity for you, just wait until you see what is in store for him in college. Of course, there are new dangers that are unique to that scene and new opportunities for the Enemy as well, but we will encounter those in due course.

College is all about freedom. It will be your job to encourage him to embrace that freedom and indulge in every hidden desire he has only tasted of while in high school. Naturally, he will see his freedom as something he rightly "deserves." He'll think his freedom has truly liberated him from the bondage of his parents' wishes. Convince him that he has earned this little foray into an "adult world," a world of glamour and excitement, one that he can leave any time he wants! What he won't see are your claws digging deeper into him with every step he takes toward his "freedom." If all goes well, by the time he exits in four (or five or six) years, he'll be entirely yours, all the while thinking he is entirely "his own man."

Ah, college. What a playground for a young demon such as yourself. However, there are a few key principles you should keep in mind in order to inflict the most damage. Do whatever you can to get him in and around potentially sinful situations: parties with plenty of alcohol, empty dorm rooms with unfiltered Internet access, late-night encounters with available college girls, you get the idea. What we have working in our favor is the inherent desire of sin itself to control these creatures. Their own Scriptures talk about it (Gen. 4:7), but they certainly don't act as though they believe it. They act brash and think they are victorious simply because the Enemy died on a tree. The war may appear to be lost, Tarflanks, but it isn't, and regardless, it doesn't mean we can't win our share of battles along the way. Get him around enough compromising situations and he's sure to be compromised eventually.

You see, humans are the most gullible creatures around (besides the puppy perhaps). We lie to them and tell them that this sin they are on the verge of embracing will be the answer to all of their problems. If they were only aware of our lies, and of the Enemy's ability to make them truly happy, they'd ignore us. But the promises of the Enemy, as you know, are often hidden, and require discipline to receive.

Remind your subject that our promises are instant, full, and require no work. Of course, they have no power to provide any lasting sustenance, but this they will not see; they are such shortsighted creatures. If you can feed his immediate passions and distract him from lingering on the deep heart longings that aren't satisfied by sin, he will become a loyal subject, to you and to Our Father Below.

Another concept that is important in this discussion is what I shall call "The Moment." One of the Enemy's followers is in a rock band and wrote a song on this theme. (I was sure he was one of ours for a while, but I think we might have lost him for good.)

It is our job to help the humans to get stuck in these moments, and then make them believe that they'll never get out of them. Now, the Enemy has promised them that he won't let them be tempted beyond what they can bear, and that He will always provide a way out (1 Cor. 10:13). Do everything in your power to hide those two facts from him. Make it look as though he has just one choice when faced with a temptation: to follow through on it. And why wouldn't he? After all, it will make him happy! If these simpletons would only realize that getting themselves out of the moment would destroy the power of temptation! But they don't.

Like I mentioned before, they seek happiness, and they believe that the moment they're stuck in is something that they can't live without. It becomes an identity issue: where are they going to get their joy from? Sin or God? Keep offering them the temporary joy of sin. And even when you don't deliver, they'll be back every time, just like a puppy dog. Remember, Tarflanks, my son, to constantly teach them to repeat the statement, "I didn't have any choice." It will serve you well in teaching them to avoid their guilt and not reflect on their unhappiness.

One more topic, and then I must turn in. It involves grace. Do what you can to pervert your patient's view of it. Don't let him see it as it is intended to be. It's meant to bring him to a view of himself where he realizes he is wretched and empty, and then with the help of the Enemy, he becomes a new creature. Make sure he doesn't have a healthy understanding of his need for the Enemy, and of his worth in His eyes. Try to stick to the extremes (this is a good tactic in most instances). On the one extreme, hope that he says: "I'm a decent fellow. I can do whatever I want, and just ask for forgiveness." What he won't realize is that grace isn't just some cosmic credit card with no limit. Eventually, he will enjoy the sinning so much that he won't bother to stop and ask for forgiveness anymore, and he'll be yours.

The other side to push him to is the belief that grace is only for the slimy, "unsaved" heathen like drug dealers and disgraced politicians. Make him believe that when he makes mistakes, no one will ever have grace for him. Christians aren't supposed to make mistakes. Make him think that he has to be perfect, and when he isn't, that he must not be a real follower of the Enemy. Encourage him to wallow in the shame of it all. This starts the downward spiral you're looking for: first he believes grace doesn't extend to him. Eventually, he will forsake showing it to others as well.

Meanwhile, steer him clear of any authentic connections with other Enemy-followers, because the moment he begins to think he has a safe place to be himself, you will have lost. Keep him far away from any real relationships where he can be himself and "open up."

I trust I will hear many good reports during your time there. Do keep me posted. If you get in a jam, you can always call my cell. Call after 9, if possible, when the minutes are free. (I'm beginning to regret Our Father's success in having "night minutes" classified as those after 9, but who am I to argue?)

Warmly,

Stankerton

LUKE'S STORY

Throughout college I was pretty intentional about growing in my faith. I was studying theology at a Christian school and was excited about all that God wanted to teach me in my college years. But one huge obstacle set me back regarding my walk with God for the second half of my college career: a relationship I entered into near the end of my sophomore year. I had been waiting for "the right one" very patiently throughout high school and decided to wait until college to date for two basic reasons: 1) lack of solid Christian options and 2) I was able to recognize through direct and indirect experiences the shallow and time-wasting nature of typical high school relationships.

My time of setback arose when I expected (practically demanded) that God come through in providing the right person for me, since I'd been patient in high school. My freshman year of college I hadn't met "the right one" and grew somewhat impatient. This impatience and lack of trust in God caused me to take matters into my own hands. Though I would never have admitted it at the time, I was clearly not "waiting on God" to bring the right person. I was infatuated and mistook that for love. This new relationship was with a brand-new Christian with a very abusive past. More than anything, this girl was in desperate need of time to grow in her faith before thinking about a serious relationship. But I was impatient and infatuated and she was interested, so we started dating.

The second (and biggest) problem came when I allowed the relationship to become physical. I hadn't even kissed anyone until this relationship and had always planned on saving my first kiss for my fiancée/wife. But one night I adjusted my boundaries *just slightly* for a very dumb reason, and you know the rest of the story. A couple months later I would be drowning in sexual addiction with a person who had been searching desperately for *real love*, not selfish lust. This sent us on a two-plus year ride of guilt, shame, frustration, and spiritual starvation. I finally became aware of how unhealthy our relationship was and I decided to end it.

Things got better when we both were eventually forced to move to new places, but the damage done to both of us remains to this day. As if all of this weren't enough, throughout this time, I developed a terrible habit of viewing women primarily through a sexual or objectifying lens. In my mind, women could easily become no more than a means to an end, even if I would never verbalize or intentionally think such disgusting things. I had conditioned myself to think of women in this way by putting my own pleasure above a sincere love for the person I was turning into an object. In the past year, God has been healing me of this view of women. My sexuality is being refined and restored, but it is not easy and the memories from my past creep in at times and make me feel like I'm back to where I started.

All of this is to say (beg rather)—please take note of all my mistakes and please learn from them. If you ever watch the movie *Requiem for a Dream,* it will make you never, ever want to take drugs. It is my hope that my story and all my mistakes will likewise be a deterrent to seeking fulfillment outside of God's guidance.

11.

FACING PLURALISM AND RELATIVISM

I could give you a hundred examples of pluralism and relativism from my university experience. Once, on the first day of a class, a history professor tallied the distance between the ends of our universe and the time that the universe has likely existed. From these enormous numbers he concluded, "In light of this, it is a bit naïve to think that our individual lives are particularly meaningful or that our small conceptions of reality are of much importance in the history of such a universe." Encouraging, isn't it?

Another time I was asked to be on an interreligious discussion panel. One young woman sitting next to me said, "I think Jesus was an amazing person, but I think everyone's religious expression is pleasing to God if it is truly sincere. We all connect with God in our own way, and we cannot say that anyone's sincere devotion is wrong. That would be arrogant." (When it was my turn to ask a question, I asked her if it was wrong for me to torture babies as worship so long as I was deeply sincere.)

Pluralism and relativism, the reigning philosophies of the American university, come in many shapes and sizes, but eventually they all come to the same philosophical bottom line: that no view, especially one that is philosophical or religious, can be inherently superior to any other. Truth is *relative*, and there are a *plural* number of valid views sufficient to answer questions concerning our lives. It is usually assumed that early in your university studies you will accept that there is simply no objective truth but only many different perspectives. Pluralism[12] teaches that our perspective is our truth, and the fact that we think our truth is *the* truth comes from the fact that we can't see that our criteria for determining truth is conditioned by the circumstances of our intellectual or social environment.

In most modern university classes it is simply unthinkable to suggest that you have *the* truth, and that to say you know "the truth" (meaning a description of reality true for everyone) is considered the height of arrogance, intolerance, and ignorance. To make matters worse, this viewpoint isn't so much *taught* as *assumed*, so one has little opportunity to bring it up for reevaluation. To do so is regarded by many as rehashing whether or not the sun goes around the earth. To most students entering the university this is not news. You have already encountered relativistic ideals in high school, media, and possibly even at church.

Understanding the allure

I think before we look at some of the biggest problems with relativism for the Christian, we need to ask, "Why is this such a popular philosophy?" What is it that draws so many very bright people to assert so absolutely that there are no absolutes? If we ask sympathetically, I think we can see several reasons.

First, exclusivism has a mixed history. People who strongly hold very definite beliefs can be harmful to the peaceful coexistence of many diverse groups in a society. Imperialists, who thought they had the truth about what civilization should be, destroyed rich primitive cultures in the age of imperialism. Religious exclusivists have killed many in the name of "God's Truth." Even atheist

12. Often throughout this chapter I will use pluralism and relativism interchangeably. In more academic writing, these two philosophies can be distinguished from one another but on the popular college level, there tends to be little, if any, distinction.

exclusivists like Pol Pot, Stalin, Hitler, and their followers have killed millions of people who have not accepted the "absolute truth" of communism, fascism, Nazism, or whatever was the hot doctrine of the day. Absolutists have destroyed peace, and such ideological clashes bring about many forms of conflict that disrupt and shorten lives. On this count we have to accept that if pluralism can bring about more peace and tolerance, it is attractive.

Second, religious exclusivism is a bold claim. To claim that the gospel is true, and that therefore the heart of other faiths is by definition not true, is very serious. It is to say that billions of people are drastically and fundamentally wrong in how they view the universe. In light of the advanced philosophies and social structures of other religious cultures that are thousands of years old, it is easy to see that exclusivism can be an audacious claim.

Third, religious exclusivism interrupts our personal desires. If we accept that there is an objective truth, then we may have to live by it. This alternative is seen by many as a despicable alternative to the complete personal freedom and individuality offered by pluralism.

Last, pluralism is the reigning opinion of the university, media, and political arena. Its popularity alone, for most people, is enough to be convincing. The view that there are many truths, and therefore, many ways to God, is sold not only by professors, but also in cartoons, films, political debates, newspaper articles, and by most other figures of authority and counterauthority.

Given this short list, we should not be surprised that the vast majority of our friends and colleagues have a pluralistic view of truth and faith. In fact, it would be presumptuous to assume that all of the readers of this book have come to the conclusion that to be a Christian means being a religious exclusivist. Therefore, before discussing how to engage pluralism constructively in a college setting, we need to see if pluralism is at all compatible with the gospel of Jesus Christ.

The exclusivity of the gospel of Christ

There have been a myriad of books written on this subject in the last thirty years; here I will give only a summary. In this section I simply want to make three observations toward demonstrating that the message of Christianity is contradictory to the teaching of contemporary pluralism in the widest possible sense. I will not be discussing specific verses of Scripture that stand clearly against a pluralist view (Jn. 14:6-7, Rom. 3:30, Eph. 4:4-6, Isa. 44:8). What is more important is for the reader to see that the big pictures of both systems are widely incompatible.

Problem one: God's narrative

The first difficulty is in what has been called the "death of the metanarrative." A metanarrative is "the big story." All of us have our own little stories, and our families make up bigger stories, but if we combined all the families and nations throughout all of history, we would have what is called a "metanarrative," the big story.

In the Christian Bible it is assumed, from the first page until the last, that history has a destiny. The human race is going somewhere, God is taking us there, and there is an inevitable climax—first in the redemption of humanity through Christ, and second, in the final elimination of evil and reunification of believers with God in His kingdom at the end of the created order. Galatians 4:4a says, "But when *the time had fully come,* God sent his Son" and later in Revelation it is clear that all things are being orchestrated to a glorious conclusion. Christianity speaks of a metanarrative from the garden to glory. It is assumed literally everywhere, on every page of the entire Bible.

In a relativistic view of history this is intolerable, because to assert the truth of this one story is to exclude a thousand other stories. If the Christian story is true, then Muslim, atheist, Hindu, and other stories are not true. Their religious interpretation of their own experience would be false, since, for example, the universe is not *both* moving in an endless cycle (as in Hinduism) and with linear destiny (as in Christianity). This has led pluralist religious philosophers to try to either merge all religions into one vague story ("all religions are basically the same") or say there is no true metanarrative, only many true narratives.

This situation forces the sincere believer to choose between the view that everyone is right (a view never considered a viable option in the disciplines of physics or math), or the view that some are right and others are wrong, which is the assumption of biblical, historical Christianity.

Problem two: Christ and sin

The second major difficulty is that pluralism destroys the problem of sin and the solution of the cross, the center and meaning of the Christian faith. Christianity (in spite of the popular view that it is simply a vague celebration of the fatherhood of God and the brotherhood of man) is a very clear and definite proposition. Biblically speaking, the problem with humanity is not a lack of education; it is not a need for an equitable distribution of resources, a better behavior alternative, the completion of a reincarnating cycle, or anything else. The problem with us is sin. Sin is the corporate and individual willful rebellion of humanity against our Creator, which manifests itself in an infinitely diverse spectrum of human emotions and behaviors. Whether the specific action is widespread genocide or garden-variety selfishness, God traces this back to a rejection of Himself as the rightful Ruler of His created order and the rejection of His "Torah," or instruction: His Law. This sin is not simply a choice, but a soul and social infection that permeates our individual lives, cultures, and nations.

In this problem, this one great common doom, Christianity alone (and historic Judaism from which it came) trumpets the true problem of our hearts. The suffering in our world and in eternity is our fault. We contaminated God's pure creation with it, and through our active wills it has been unleashed upon us. God responds to this in two ways.

First, He responds to our sin in righteous anger. Romans 6:23 says, "For the wages of sin is death," and in Scripture, God always means more than simply the destruction of our bodies. So the great dilemma of humanity, according to the Christian faith, is that all mankind is dead twice—at the hands of our own sin, and at the receiving end of the righteous and deserved wrath of God Himself. If one accepts that this is what the Bible teaches, then the Christian faith stands completely separate in its assessment of the problem religion must solve—the problem of sin and the righteous wrath of God. Yet, from this desperate problem comes the most unlikely and unique answer. It is that through Christ's death, God saved us from ourselves and from our just punishment.

God's second response to sin is love. God unifies these two conflicting perfections (wrath and love) in the cross. Romans 3:26 states: "He [God] did it [the cross] . . . so as to *be just* and the one who justifies *those who have faith in Jesus.*" The Christian gospel says that through our belief in Jesus Christ, God credits our deserved punishment to Jesus and Christ's righteousness to us. Furthermore, He demonstrates His love by giving us the greatest of all gifts—Himself. Through the righteousness we receive in Christ, we can have a relationship with God, and reenter into a faithful relationship with the King of the universe. Our treason is put away, and a new loving relationship is begun. The death and resurrection of Christ accomplishes more than just this, of course. It signals the victory of good over evil, of light over darkness. It breaks the curse that Adam brought on the human race with his rebellion in the garden. But perhaps more than anything, it is God's sign to His people that their sin problem has been dealt with.

With this demonstrated, it is important to understand that the New Testament clearly portrays the cross of Christ as the only solution to our sin problem. There are then, by definition, no other ways to God if sin is the problem and this is the only proposed solution.

If you are inclined to think there are many ways to God, think for a moment on how small this makes of the work of Jesus. If you were God, would you empty yourself of all power and glory that is rightfully yours, face the limitation of becoming a baby, live humbly as a poor peasant, face the constant disrespect of small-minded men, and finally die the most humiliating and painful death ever devised by man to simply create another way to God?

Jesus assumes the opposite of this in Mark 14:35–36, "Going a little farther, he [Jesus] fell to the ground and prayed that if possible the hour [His imminent death] might pass from him. 'Abba, Father,' he said, 'everything is possible for you. Take this cup from me. Yet not what I will, but what you will.' " Do you see the problem? At that moment, Jesus didn't want to go through the agony of the cross. Even in His resolute divinity His humanity knew the high physical and emotional cost of this saving work. Would you do this just to accumulate *yet another* path to God modern people might choose if they were so inclined? Paul says in Galatians 2:19–21:

For through the law I died to the law so that I might live for God. I have been crucified with Christ and I no longer live, but Christ lives in me. The life I live in the body, I live by faith in

> the Son of God, who loved me and gave him-
>
> self for me. I do not set aside the grace of God,
>
> for if righteousness could be gained through
>
> the law, Christ died for nothing!

Do you see the point? God himself had already given the perfect law! If there were any other way to come to God, then surely it would be by the Law. Yet Paul says with complete conviction and clarity that if there were any other way to receive righteousness from God to save us from the unrighteousness of our sin, then Christ died for nothing. The glorious center of Christianity is the cross: God making a single way, Himself, at unthinkable cost, when we could never make any way ourselves.

Problem three: The Bible

Third, and last in our tiny discussion, is the place of the Scriptures in the Christian message. The Bible, within itself and throughout the history of the church, has always been understood as revelation *from God*. That is not to say we deny the human authorship of the biblical texts, but we believe these writers were inspired divinely in the writing. This is not, as some modern scholars have suggested, a later understanding of the Scriptures, but is quite clear from within the text of the Bible itself and the earliest writings of the Christian church.

Within a pluralist framework, there are *no* divinely inspired texts of this sort, but only religious people who have responded in writing to their religious experiences. At first, it is possible to see this as an unimportant distinction, but I assure you it is not. The former view assumes that the Bible is primarily a successful communication of God to man of the truth about Himself. The latter assumes the Scriptures are communications by human persons about their religious feelings and experiences, which may or may not have been interpreted accurately. The result is that, within a pluralist framework, Scripture is not a successful communication from God, but rather one of many texts written by humans about their intellectual and emotional religious experiences.

Once this is the case you can see how pluralists might search different religions for some underlying similarities and then, based on those similarities, assert that all religions were getting at the same basic experience, and that they were therefore all equally true. This is the opposite of the Christian view of Scripture, and Christian Scripture is at the very center of the historic definition of the gospel and the daily practice of our faith.

Hopefully you can now see that pluralism and Christianity are propositions opposed to each other on the most basic level and assumptions. To unify these two worldviews is to most certainly kill one of them.

Some strategy points

With the problem stated, there are three pieces of advice fitting for a student who wants to make a difference for Christ on her university campus. None of these is an easy answer, but sooner or later we all learn that there are no shortcuts to the cultivation and reproduction of authentic Christ-following faith.

First, shut up and listen. This is universally true, but especially true concerning your professors. Most Christian college students know what pluralism and relativism are in theory, but you must study them seriously before attacking them. It is sheer folly for you to open your mouth too soon. Not only will your argument probably stink, but you will also come off as arrogant (the preeminent sin in pluralist culture), and you will likely be disrespectful. So listen and ask questions, of your professors and of your friends.

You are not Socrates, trying to tie people in knots by your questions. You are exploring their views yourself, and learning something about the minds you are trying to reach for Christ. People in your classes are not your personal "projects." They are people with stories for whom Christ willfully spilled His blood and wants to save. To understand, love, and ultimately convince the modern university student, you must listen—listen long, and listen carefully. Besides, most people are not ready to listen until they have first been heard.

Second, to beat a sage you have to be a sage. C.S. Lewis has said, "Good philosophy must exist, if for no other reason than because bad philosophy must be answered." Jesus Christ came to save whole humans: body, soul, and mind. If you endeavor to save only the soul and not transform the mind, in the long run you will not see even the soul saved, in either yourself or others. You must think and think hard. You simply cannot make a difference in combating the great intellectual idol of our time with a mediocre, fat mind. There is no alternative to wisdom and thoughtfulness, and it is a necessary part of biblical Christianity. I recommend starting by simply reading your Bible more carefully. What is it saying? What claims is it making about reality? Then, read other good books. And not just popular bestsellers but well-written classics.

Third, learn to deal shrewdly with pluralist rhetoric. At first it may seem daunting, but stick with it. Learning right answers is not the same thing as learning how to give effective answers; a sage must learn to do both. To minister in this setting you will need to study the answers and, just as important, learn how to give answers so people can hear them. It takes time and effort, but it will bear fruit for the rest of your life.

12.

SURVIVING A CHRISTIAN SCHOOL

There is nothing like Christian colleges in the entire world. They exist as somewhat utopian islands in a sea of reality in that you will never again in all your life be completely surrounded by so many Christians at one time. This is not a bad thing by any means, but you must recognize that those of you headed to a Christian college will be encountering an environment that is unique. And with it come unique opportunities and challenges.

You all have different reasons for choosing a Christian school over a secular one. Let me list some good ones, followed by some bad ones.

Good reason #1: Your parents have offered to pay only if you attend a Christian school. Hard to argue with free college.

Good reason #2: You are a newer Christian, or your faith is somewhat shaky, and you know that if you go to a secular university, it will not be strong enough to last. It's important for you to be honest enough with yourself to know this, and to act on it.

Good reason #3: You have a deep desire to use your college years to learn from a Christian perspective, and feel that you will be stifled if taught from a secular point of view. One of the best advantages of a Christian school is the Christian professors who can impact you. Make sure you take advantage of those opportunities to be mentored and taught by godly men and women whose lives you wish to emulate. However, don't turn your brain off either, because even at some prestigious Christian universities, there are teachers who have drifted into questionable and unorthodox doctrines.

Good reason #4: Your primary goal for college is to spend your time seriously studying the Bible. Having an entire semester-long class on the Old or New Testaments can have a profound effect on individuals in shaping how they view, interpret, and understand the Bible. Unless you go to seminary, you may not have this kind of chance later on in life, even if you go to church every Sunday.

And now for some bad reasons:

Bad reason #1: You really want to find a good Christian spouse and think this is the only way to do it. Please. As though God can't provide for this except through a Christian school. God is bigger than that, and can bring you the right person wherever you go. Years ago, one of my students cited this very reason for his decision to attend a Christian college. The irony? He started dating a phenomenal Christian girl from his hometown the summer before he left for college, and married her six years later.

Bad reason #2: You are looking for some good Christian fellowship. If this is your only reason for going, you need to know that a Christian campus is not the only place to find this. Groups like InterVarsity and Cru can meet these needs well.

Bad reason #3: You don't want to deal with sinful people. The problem is that sin is just as prevalent at a Christian school, but it might not be apparent at the surface. And guess what? The world is a sinful place, so you might as well get used to it in college.

In light of some of these reasons, then, I have for you a list of three don'ts and three dos as you head off to a Christian campus.

Don't think everyone there is Christian

Christian colleges are notorious for the group of supposedly Christian students who have been sent there by their parents, but who are the furthest thing from Christian possible.

They are finally free of their parents' rigidity and are looking to exercise their freedom to indulge their sinful nature. And they will be looking for some friends to join them in their revelry. Other students may have every intention of wanting to avoid sin, but will struggle with it.

Christian college students have premarital sex. They drink alcohol and use drugs. Christian college students watch pornography, cheat on tests, and are mean to people. Why? Because they're sinners, and sin is powerful. Be careful that you don't let your guard down because you assume that everyone's a Christian, or because you think your campus is a sin-free zone. And if you find *yourself* in a cycle of hidden sin, remember that the only way out is by bringing that sin into the light.

A final, related note on this point. On at least one Christian college campus, I've heard the acronym **NCMO** being thrown around. It stands for "noncommittal make out." That's when two friends (usually it's already a "hazy" relationship as discussed in chapter 2) find themselves alone together and they make out. No wondering "what this means," no DTR (define the relationship) talks, just good ol'-fashioned tonsil hockey. This seems so obvious, so I'll keep my comments to one sentence. Don't kid yourself into thinking this is something that honors God.

Don't judge

In light of the above, you also must be careful that you refrain from judging others and their walk with the Lord. Keep in mind that it is *His* job to grow them and convict them of sin, not yours. It will be tempting to want to have impossibly high standards for everyone around you, which no one can live up to. This then leads you to hypocrisy, since you won't be able to live up to these standards either. Have the same grace for others that you would hope them to have for you. And if you have a problem with someone, don't gossip about them. Either pray for them, or if you feel it is appropriate, confront them.

Don't let the school *be* your relationship with God

It is not your school's primary job to help you grow spiritually while you are there. Rather, its job is to teach you from a Christian perspective. It will be very easy, then, for you to become complacent about pursuing God because it will feel as though you are always talking *about* God. This cannot replace your worship of God or your interaction *with* God himself. Don't let your four years of college become an intellectual exercise. Pursue God with the same passion you would no matter where you are. This means that personal Bible study and prayer (aka "the quiet time") will still be incredibly important for you.

Just because you've been studying the Bible in your Bible classes doesn't mean it's been feeding your soul. An analogy I heard in relation to this compares the Bible to a love letter. It's one thing to examine a love letter for its content, studying it, diagramming the sentences, parsing the verbs, and drawing conclusions from it. It's quite another thing to take it, go away alone, smell it, and then read it with the passion with which it was intended. Don't let your love relationship with God grow stale.

Do find a way to get around those far from God

If you never cross paths with a non-Christian while you're in college, you will lose touch with reality and you'll very easily lose any passion you ever had for seeing them reconciled to God. So figure out how to get around them.

Studying at the same place off-campus will help this. You could also try to get involved with a Young Life chapter nearby, or with your church's youth group. Or find a job off-campus. It is easy for the Christian campus to become a bubble, where you are insulated from the rest of the world.

A helpful analogy related to this is comparing your spiritual growth to eating, and your ministry with others to exercising. At a Christian school, it will be easy for you to do a whole lot of eating. But if you don't exercise, you run the risk of getting spiritually fat. We were made to be spiritually lean! There must be a balance, which can be achieved by getting yourself around nonbelievers.

Do find a church

The joke among many Chicago Christian university students is that they attend Pillow Creek, as opposed to Willow Creek, a large church in the suburbs. Meaning: they sleep in on Sunday mornings. Especially for those of you that have mandatory chapel three times a week, getting up for church on a Sunday will seem unnecessary and redundant. Fight this urge and find a church. You may want to go church shopping with friends or roommates so that when you find one, you can help each other get there. Consider serving at a church in their children's or youth ministries as a way to connect.

Do have a sense of humor

This won't be an issue for all of you, but the tendency for some will be to have an ultra-serious attitude in all they do. I encountered this problem when I was in seminary. Yes, studying the truths of God should be sobering, but they needn't always be grave and solemn. You will find that if you take yourself too seriously, life itself will become too heavy for you to handle. Remember to laugh.

Not everyone has a great experience at a Christian college, and the same can be true for a secular one. The key to your success lies mostly in how you respond to what they have to offer.

JACKIE'S STORY

After graduating from high school, I attended a large public university in the Midwest. In high school I was a student leader at my youth group and had a strong group of Christian friends who were always around me. I was nervous that I would have a hard time finding this connection at such a large public school. However, the week before classes started there were several organizations around campus, on the quad between buildings, and even in the residence halls that were setting up booths for new students to get involved. There were hundreds of different groups to get involved in, and about 5 to 6 large Christian organizations. During this first week I made it a point to go and talk with each Christian organization to get a feel for the community, their style of worship, and how they ran small groups. Most of these organizations had a worship service once a week, as well as small groups that met midweek. I tried to attend each of these groups for the first month, and then finally chose one organization where I felt I could get plugged in.

Throughout my freshman year, I met some Christian friends and also participated in a small group. I found that being a Christian at a large university was not as scary or isolating as I thought it might be. But during my sophomore year I realized that I didn't agree with the philosophy of ministry behind the group I had chosen. For instance, this group tended to favor "closed" small groups, whereas I preferred small groups that were open to newcomers. I wish I had spoken up earlier about how I felt, because I later found out that the rest of the girls in my group felt the same way and we all ended up leaving the group at different times.

After I stopped going to the small group, I became more involved with the church that I had been attending. Once I put more energy into going to church, I realized how many opportunities they had, both at church and in the community, things like volleyball and softball games that I could invite friends to. They also emphasized serving in a practical way. I was able to join a work project that helped build houses and clean up local parks. I also loved being around people of all different ages (babies, students, parents, grandparents) rather than just being around college students 24/7. I think it helped show me how people can be involved and grow with a church at all different ages. Ultimately what I realized is that some people will thrive in on-campus groups (which I certainly did my first year), some may prefer a church off-campus, while others will enjoy both.

Since graduation it has still been very important to me to find a church and get involved with it. Not every church is the same and not every Christian organization is the same. But God will guide you, and if you're open, will lead you to the place that will nourish you spiritually.

13.

FINDING BALANCE

Picture the following scenarios: You are trying to share about Jesus with a friend in your dorm and you are having a very open and intelligent discussion about the historical and philosophical claims of Christianity. Another student on your floor, a known Christian, walks into the lounge and interjects, "You know, Paul called the gospel 'foolishness to the wise'; you two are just over-thinking this . . . (turns to your friend) . . . you have to just believe." How do you respond?

You and a new Christian friend are leading a Bible study in a nearby dorm for a group that is studying 2 Corinthians. You read 6:17 which says, " 'Come out from them and be separate,' says the Lord. 'Touch no unclean thing and I will receive you.' " Someone asks what that means and another person says, "I think it's clear that Paul is saying that Christians shouldn't associate with unbelievers because they will corrupt our faith." The first student looks a little confused, but nods. You say?

You are sitting in the dining hall with two other Christians. One begins to talk about her depression, and how she is struggling to find joy right now. The other student encourages her by saying, "You know, emotions aren't really a big part of real faith. We're Christians, and that is really about focusing on our duty and responsibility, not on emotions." After he finishes, she looks at you.

Here are three practical examples of everyday college life that are in need of some theological reflection. Are you ready for situations like this? Do you have a Game Plan for thinking theologically, or are you going to wait until things get personal?

A panorama of excesses

The problem in each of the examples above is that something is out of balance. Whether it is emotions excluding the intellect, an immediate application of Scripture excluding proper investigation of its meaning, or stoicism excluding proper emotions, we all struggle to think and feel and live well for Jesus in a balanced way.

All of life has deficiencies and extremes that need to be actively avoided. Likewise, in Christian experience there are also unhelpful excesses. Sometimes their effect is minimal, and in some cases these extremes amount to apostasy (the state where a person or group no longer holds to the very minimums of biblical-historical Christianity). Although there are a thousand different particular excesses to avoid, most of them boil down to four main categories: emotionalism (excessive mysticism), rationalism, traditionalism, and literalism.

Before we look at how each of these four extremes can be balanced, it is important to note that each excess exists because someone wanted to rightly avoid some real deficiency. Many a Christian starts out with noble intentions for his solution to "what's wrong with the world," but enthusiasm for that solution can easily lead him off course to an equally inappropriate answer. He is like the person who grows obese as an adult because in his childhood he was so poor he nearly starved. From this basic pendulum, swinging from one extreme to another, almost all Christian excesses flow.

Hence the believer must find a middle course between Jesus's disgust of half-heartedness and the corresponding danger of unbalanced fanaticism.

The Wesleyan Quadrilateral

It is our task to use all of the tools God has given us to understand what it means to live as Christians, and to engage all our faculties in Christ's service. Yet it is hard to be full of emotion without being emotional, traditional without becoming dated, reasonable without becoming rationalistic, and scriptural without being literalistic. I have personally found the greatest help integrating these four areas in the writings of John Wesley, through his method known as the "Wesleyan Quadrilateral."

John Wesley lived, much like us, in a time of rationalism, emotionalism, traditionalism, and literalism. During his ministry he fought against the unbiblical mysticism of some of the Moravians and other groups, worked in the sometimes stodgy traditionalism of the eighteenth-century Church of England, and reasoned against the rationalism of the Deists/Empiricists and the literalism of some Calvinist and Anabaptist extremists. As Wesley tried to be faithful to Christ amidst this outside pressure, he consistently used four authorities (hence the name "quadrilateral") to form a faithful, dynamic, and healthy theology.

Scripture

Scripture was Wesley's first and final authority. He believed, unlike the rationalists, that Scripture stood in judgment of him and that reason was to be used to make sense of the Scriptures and not to build skepticism towards them. Although he brought other authorities to the table, when in conflict, Scripture had the final authority.

Reason

Second, Wesley believed that the Christian must have a *high view of reason*. The Bible alone is not an easy book, but even more difficult is finding a synthesis between our experiences, tradition, and the Bible. To this task Wesley committed his mind passionately for the duration of his life. Wesley would flatly reject the position that religion was something one could "think too much about," or that the spiritual was not meant to be analyzed by the rational. God has seen fit to make spiritual beings rational, and He has sovereignly and intentionally intertwined the mystical with the rational and historical.

Tradition

Third, Wesley was a great lover of *tradition,* by which he meant the creeds of the Christian church and the writings of the "authoritative" church fathers. He believed that if you were creative enough to make up a new doctrine, you were creative enough to be a heretic. It was not that he was against engaging new generations with new ways of talking about the faith; it was that he saw how arrogant it was to try to interpret Scripture and faith completely within our immediate cultural and historical situation.

An ear to tradition protects us from the errors of the past, alerts us to cultural blind spots today, and gives us a sense of grandeur and history in our Christian experience. Christian movements that have neglected the legions of tradition have often become heretical, ethnocentric, and culturally dominated instead of culturally transforming. As G.K. Chesterton has said, "neglect of history will make us merely men of our times."

Experience

Last, even in the midst of destructive emotionalism, Wesley never allowed himself to marginalize the importance of *emotion and experience* in the Christian life. Although Wesley did not define his theology based on experience, he saw experience as an important diagnostic for faith. If our faith doesn't work in experience, we probably have something wrong somewhere. When Wesley saw his theology didn't work in the practice of his own life, or the lives of others, he allowed himself to be driven back to Scripture, tradition, and reason to rethink his conclusions. The attention he paid to emotions and experience kept Wesley's faith fresh and his message relevant.

Our present need

Although this may all sound a lot like what you might learn in a college theology class (you should be so fortunate as to take one!), I assure you that having a practical and systematic way to think theologically is of the highest practical importance. First, because of the interdenominational nature of most college ministries, you will meet people from all kinds of different Christian backgrounds, and it is important that you have some means of evaluating the differences you find in your campus's Christian community. Having these four things on your mental radar screen can help you learn from and connect with people from all of these different groups.

For example, when I was in college I was quite convinced that the true mode of Christian baptism was the immersion of believers. As I read the Bible I saw believers getting dunked. "Who could deny it?" I thought, and I looked on people who believed in infant baptism with a certain amount of suspicion. However, I found to my horror while in seminary that in the two thousand years of church history my view was held by none of the church fathers, none of the Reformers, and very few people at all until the last three or four hundred years.

Did I change my view on baptism? Not really. I still believe the bulk of biblical evidence points toward my original view, but my disposition toward my Christian brothers and sisters who practice infant baptism has changed dramatically. Seeing their view as the majority opinion in the history of the church, and understanding their biblical and experiential reason for the practice, helped me to no longer look on them with such suspicion.

Avoiding extremes without achieving mediocrity

I wish balanced or "holistic" Christianity were really as simple as just seeking a middle ground in our views, being "centrist," but it isn't. Hiding in the middle of a theological spectrum is about as safe as being in the middle of a crowd, or as Kierkegaard used to say, a "mob." There is nothing inherently safe about being a fanatic or a moderate. Hitler was a fanatic, but so were the apostle Paul, Gandhi, and Martin Luther King Jr. And though we may say Abraham Lincoln found greatness as a moderate, we can say the opposite of Pontius Pilate's attempt to be a moderate.

The reason that getting beyond mere "moderation" is important is that there is a kind of balance that is its own dangerous extreme. When a person seeks balance, she often uses primarily the faculty of reason and tries to objectively and dispassionately examine the extremes around her, attempting to bring them together into a logically unified whole. This, in my view, is a noble and important step along the road to wisdom. However, it is a short step from being an observer of all life to becoming *merely* an observer of it. It is one thing to think carefully about life; it is quite another to only think about it and not engage our passions in concrete action. The head must move the heart, and the heart must activate the body.

Someone who is constantly talking about his "balanced" and sophisticated philosophy, yet does so with neither passion nor action may well be a first-rate philosopher, but he is likely not a Christian. Jesus said in Mark 12:30, "Love the Lord your God with all your heart and with all your soul and with all your mind and with all your strength." It is not good enough to use only one of these faculties, no matter how balanced our use of it. So biblical, holistic Christian faith must take seriously all of our human faculties (emotions, physical strength, intellect), not just balance all of the relevant information that comes to us in Scripture, theology, tradition, and experience.

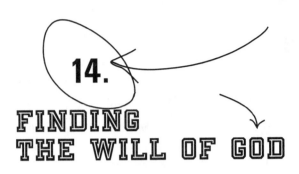

14.

FINDING
THE WILL OF GOD

God told me to pray for you last night. God told me to marry that girl over there. God is leading me to go on a mission trip to Uzbekistan. I just don't have a peace about this. These types of phrases are heard regularly in Christian circles, and they can be extremely intimidating. Is this the way God speaks to all of us, all the time? Am I missing something if God doesn't speak to me like this?

There can be a lot of confusion when it comes to how we find the will of God. And for many of us, it may feel like God is like a sneaky card hawk on the street corner, daring us to guess which card is the ace of spades. Wrong! You've lost! You are now currently walking outside of my will, but thanks for playing!

A life of "being led"

The book of Acts sets an example of the Holy Spirit's leading people in specific ways. In chapter sixteen, we hear first that the Holy Spirit guides Paul away from the province of Asia, then urges him in a dream to travel to Macedonia and share the gospel there. In the book of John, Jesus says He does only what he sees His Father doing. We read in the book of Galatians about keeping in step with the Spirit. Are we to conclude, then, that our very steps should be guided carefully by the direct leading of the Holy Spirit in all we do?

During my late high school/early college years, I went through a time of confusion about this concept. I remember hearing one of my youth leaders talk about how he felt the Lord leading him while he was driving to make a left turn at a light, even though he didn't need to turn left. And he said he fought with God, but decided he wanted to be obedient, so he did it. I also heard other stories where God asked people to do foolish things, like putting a piece of an extension cord in their pocket and walk around their church. And when people asked them why, they were just supposed to say: I don't know; God just told me to do this.

After reading about how Paul was led in the way he was, and then about how God told Ezekiel to lie on his side for a long time (Ezek. 4) and for Hosea to marry a prostitute (Hos. 1), I concluded that I must be missing something. I vowed that I wanted to live radically for God, to not walk outside of His will, and so I decided to not make any decisions without knowing that God was guiding me in that direction. When I was leading music for a retreat, for instance, I wouldn't choose a certain song unless I specifically "felt a peace" about it. When I was driving or walking around, I tried to be sensitive to the ways in which God might be leading me. If God wanted me to make a left turn instead of a right, or if God wanted me to sit at this table instead of that one, I would not be disobedient.

To my surprise, this didn't bring me freedom. Rather, it plunged me into a life of confusion and fear. I was struck with the realization that I could be walking outside of God's will, and that if I didn't listen hard enough, I could be missing something. I was also greatly disappointed on one occasion when I felt certain God was leading me to live in a certain dorm the following year. I was planning on working with my school's University Ministry in the dorm I was currently in, but one night I thought I felt God tell me that I should live in a different dorm, one I really didn't want to live in. I wasn't sure, but since it was something I didn't want to do, I figured it must be God speaking to me!

I'll obey, I thought. After telling the University Ministry of my plans, I went to sign up for the dorm I thought God was leading me to live in. Much to my consternation, that dorm was full. The only one left was the one I was originally planning on living in. I was left confused and embarrassed.

The lessons

The first lesson I needed to learn was that where the Spirit of the Lord is, there is freedom (2 Cor. 3:17). This way of living couldn't have been from the Spirit of God because I felt only bondage, not freedom.

Second, I came to realize that God won't regularly think of the worst thing He has for me, and then make me do it. God is about giving you the desires of your heart (Ps. 37:4). In the dorm room situation, I think I pretty much thought: where is the last place I want to live? Then God must want me to live there. What a skewed understanding of God I had!

This doesn't mean that God never asks us to do things we don't want to do, but we shouldn't dream up the worst-case scenarios and then expect that God will ask us to do them. I remember another time in my early Christian confusion when I hung up the phone after talking with an old female friend, and had the thought: what if God tells me to marry this girl? I mean, she's nice, she loves God, and we get along OK. But I'm not attracted to her, and I don't want to marry her! But if you say to, God, I'll obey. . . . NO! God will not make you marry someone you don't want to. In fact, in my experience, if God asks you to do something you don't initially want to do, He will change your heart so that you do.

I think the Bible means it when it says that God will give us the desires of our heart. Notice that it doesn't say: He will make you want what He wants. He really does grant you your heart's wishes, *when they are godly desires.* This doesn't mean that every desire we have is a good one. I have sinful desires every day that God does not desire to give me. My point is simply that God regularly uses our heart's desires to guide us.

When we're wrong

The time when this is most dangerous, too, is when we're wrong. When Heidi's mom was in an ice-skating accident that left her in a coma, while she was in the hospital, a well-intentioned friend told Heidi that during a prayer time she felt God say that Heidi's mom would be healed. At the time, it was an encouragement to all of us to keep praying, hopeful for a full recovery. Two weeks later, though, Heidi's mom died. What were we to think then? Did we do something wrong? God wanted to heal, but we didn't have the faith? I have seen this same scenario played out in other situations, and it often leads to a great deal of disappointment.

Feel free to politely disagree with anyone who tries to tell you that God always wants to heal, that we have to claim the victory in Jesus, and it's ours. It sounds great on paper, but it doesn't always play out that way. Even when Jesus was here He didn't heal every person He met, and even those He did heal eventually died. We should pray for everyone to be healed and let God sort out the specifics; don't claim to speak for God on this topic.

A better way

So how does He lead us? A Bible verse that has been life-changing for me in more ways than one is Proverbs 16:9: "In his heart, a man plans his course, but the LORD determines his steps." This passage is such an encouragement to me. What it tells me is that I make my decisions and have my plans, but God is completely in control. As long as I am not actively disobeying Him, I have the freedom to make wise choices, and I can trust in God to bring about His will, even through my free choices. How does that work exactly? I don't have to know. I simply have to trust that God will use my free choices to bring about His will.

Another verse that brings great comfort and freedom is Psalm 84:11b: "no good thing does he withhold from those whose walk is blameless." As long as my walk is blameless (not perfect, but humble and desiring God's best), I never have to worry if I am going to be missing out on anything good that God has for me.

God and my car

This truth played out practically in my life when I went to buy a second car for our family a number of years ago. I went to a local dealership and told the guy my ballpark price range. He showed me a '91 Honda Civic, and since pastors like me are notorious for not wanting to overbuy, I thought: this is perfect. It would get me from point A to point B, and it's a Honda, so it will run forever. I told him I would come back the next day to buy it, but he wasn't going to be working then, so I said I'd see him the following day. I gave him my credit card number to put down $500 as a deposit.

On the day in-between, I prayed: Lord, this seems like a good deal and the right car for us, but if this isn't the car we're supposed to have, just show me. As usual, I received no visions or e-mails from God, so I went back as I promised to pick up and pay for the car. I walked in and the salesman said: "You're gonna kill me. They sold your car yesterday." WHAT?! What do you mean? No, I'm not gonna kill you,

I'm gonna leave and never come back. I was frustrated. Apparently, on his day off, another salesman was able to sell the car for $2000 more than what I was going to pay, so the manager authorized it.

The guy clearly felt bad, so he quickly went to his files to find another car. I was steaming and confused. He found a '93 Toyota Camry, said it was a great car, and we took it for a ride. This was a really nice car, solid and roomy, with cruise control and a sunroof. It was much nicer than the Civic, and still in our price range. I bought it, and drove it for eleven years. From my perspective, in my heart, I was planning my steps, making the best, wisest decision I could. And in essence, God said: "Hey, you know what? You could have the Civic. But you'll like this better. Enjoy it." So he ordered my steps, all to bless me.

Do not draw any further conclusions than this. I'm not saying that God wants us to always drive nice cars, or that God will only give us things that we like, or that anything bad that happens to us is from the devil. All I'm saying is that we can make decisions with freedom, knowing that God is ordering our steps, and always has our best interests in mind.

What is the will of God?

There's a different way of looking at this, a more holistic way. Nic and I both feel strongly that the Bible calls us to live lives of wisdom. The worship song "Lord, You Are More Precious Than Silver" uses biblical language to talk about the worth of God, but do you know what the original usage of that imagery was for? Wisdom. From Proverbs 3:13–15:

> Blessed is the man who finds wisdom,
>
> the man who gains understanding,

for she is more profitable than silver

and yields better returns than gold.

She is more precious than rubies;

nothing you desire can compare with her.

Nothing you desire can compare with her! The book of Proverbs goes on to speak fervently about how we should desire such wisdom. "Get wisdom, get understanding!" it tells us. The book then goes on to contrast wisdom with folly or foolishness. We each have two paths ahead of us, to seek after foolishness or wisdom.

So how, practically, does this work? One of the first and most important concepts in this regard is the fact that you as a college student are very young and are therefore not very wise. There's an expression my dad used to use regularly about me: "often wrong, but never in doubt." I'd say this describes a lot of eighteen-year-olds with freshly minted high school diplomas. The reality is that you will never be as smart in your whole life as you are right now. Once you step foot in college, you begin the process of realizing that you actually *know* very little. And the sooner you decide to start seeking after wisdom, the better off you'll be.

Often, this just involves the simple act of keeping your mouth quiet and learning from those that have gone before you. There's a reason why Proverbs calls gray hair the splendor of the old: it's a sign that they have lived more and know more than you. Take advantage of opportunities to learn from people who are older and therefore wiser than you.

Some hear more than others

I do believe that there are certain people who genuinely hear God's voice more than the rest of us. If you are one of those people, be careful how you communicate this, using phrases like: "God said, 'Do this,' and I said, 'But God,' and He said. . . ." As though God is sitting in the room, and you're chatting over coffee. I don't doubt that this is sometimes how God communicates. But be careful how you express that to others. It's more helpful to say, if you must, "I feel like God is saying. . . ." This is not a lack of faith; rather, it leaves room for human error.

Ultimately, I firmly believe that God guides us in a number of different ways. I am convinced that He sometimes sends us serendipitous events that have a distinctively divine touch, which should be received as a gift from our Father in heaven who loves us. But in terms of direct leading, our understanding of His guiding will be seen more clearly after the fact than before. However, throughout our daily lives we should have the freedom to make decisions from hearts that seek after wisdom, continually open to how God might guide us along the way, seeking sage advice from godly counsel, and trusting in a loving God to lead us where our hearts' desires are.

JUSTIN'S STORY

My freshman year, I roomed with my best friend from back home. He was a sophomore, so he showed me the ropes and introduced me to his friends. It was nice to have a group of friends when I got there, but they weren't exactly the Christian friends I had in high school. I did end up getting involved with a Christian group on campus pretty early on and met some cool guys there too.

Unfortunately, I ended up living two different lives. It only took a few months before I started drinking with some of my friends. I was still doing the Christian thing, but I kept that separate. It all unraveled right before my junior year. My girlfriend of over two years broke up with me, and my life started to take a downward spiral.

Then God stepped in. I was living with Christian guys at the time of the breakup. After a weekend of partying and drinking, I was feeling as empty as I ever had. My roommates came around me and it was then that I saw Christ as the most important thing in my life. It was amazing to see God work in my life and draw me back to him through brokenness. I was blessed to play a part in some of my friends committing their lives to Christ too.

Now I look back at my college experience and three things stand out. First, I feel like I wasted the first two years, where I could have been growing in my faith and ministering to people around me. Second, community meant the world to me. Without Christian community I don't know where I would have turned during that time of brokenness. I had to make a conscious choice to let people into my life to encourage me and hold me accountable. I had Christian friends, but it was all surface-level relationships. Finally, I realized that I could only make a difference in other people's lives if it started with my own life. Until I put my own walk with Jesus front and center, my impact was minimal. I had to decide who I wanted to be before I decided what I wanted to do. Instead, I let others decide that for me. Don't fall into that trap!

15.

WHAT YOU SHOULD KNOW ABOUT MONEY

Many, many people regret the financial choices they make in college. That's the bad news. Here's the good news: most confess they made those mistakes because they weren't paying close enough attention. Amy, a bright young Chicago girl, got her heart set on becoming a UW Badger. She got a great education but ended up with $60K in debt from paying out-of-state tuition fees.

Rachel went to an Ivy League school and studied European history. She got a great education, but she left with huge bills and low employability. She may be the most believable character at a local Renaissance Fair, but she just finished paying her last student loan bill at age thirty-five.

Another intelligent friend studied philosophy. It made him a more tedious husband to argue with but didn't create the job opportunities he needs as a father now. Another young man was deciding between two Christian colleges with a $20,000 difference in annual tuition. Should the price difference make the difference? If you think about money, are you selling out as someone "only motivated by money"? Should you only study vocational subjects like nursing, biology, business, or education?

It's our hope for you to avoid the discouragement and depression that college graduates sometimes feel from the price tag shock of what they spent during their college years. I pastor these twenty-somethings in my church. They talk to me about the embarrassment they feel that they're bringing so much debt into a marriage. They're discouraged by how many years it will take to pay off their debt. And counselors tell us that disputes about money, especially debt, are the most ongoing, irresolvable, and resentment-filled arguments couples have. Oh, and if you're hoping to get married, remember, you don't just have to pay off your own debt—you have to pay off your spouse's also. And s/he may not be getting good financial advice right now.

The seemingly unfair thing is that in your early adulthood you are going to make one of the biggest purchases you will ever make. That's a good reason to make sure it's a worthwhile investment. It's a good reason to get advice from wise people. And for what it's worth, we are going to offer ours.

Concerning debt: Know the difference

There are two main kinds of debt for our purposes: consumer debt and investment debt. Consumer debt comes from buying things that don't generate income or grow in value over time. These are called "depreciating assets"—and almost all assets are depreciating assets. Investment debt is debt that grows your financial worth over time either because it generates income or grows in value. By spending the money now to make more later, you are investing. The key is to know what is really an investment, and what is not. We want to avoid consumer debt through frugality and self-discipline, and sometimes choose investment debt when it is wise.

Financial educators affirm three kinds of legitimate investment debts. The three universally accepted investment debts are:

1. Buying a modest primary residence
2. Getting an income-generating degree
3. Executing an "approved" business plan

True investment debts, over the long term, make us able to pay the debt and make more money for our own use. Investment debts are worth making.

The biggest danger with consumer debt is getting in it in the first place. We need to hate being in debt, and work hard to avoid it. Scripture teaches that we should be working hard to have a surplus to share with others (Eph. 4:28)—not a shortage from our overspending. Debt always costs you more than you could imagine. You lose money as your purchase loses value, plus you're paying interest, plus you are losing the investment you could have made with what you spent. You are also losing emotional security, opportunities to help others, and decision-making freedom that people have when money issues are squared away.

The biggest dangers with investment debt are overspending and wishful thinking. Education is one of the easiest things on which to overspend. Tuition is not strictly governed by market forces, so prices can be artificially inflated. One evidence of this is that at most schools, all the majors cost the same amount of tuition, yet each major produces a different projected income and the departments are of varying levels of quality. The same college may be underpriced in what it charges for one major, yet dramatically overpriced in what it charges for another. It can do this partly because it is not selling to customers that think that out very often. Just because you need a college education, and you may have selected a major, doesn't mean you need to pay whatever any particular college is asking. The name of the college you attended does matter, but it does not matter nearly as much as you might think or as much as the college's promoters apparently want you to think. Ask yourself: if I go here, am I going to be overpaying for this education? How is that price tag going to affect my life for the next ten to fifteen years?

Wishful thinking comes in when we convince ourselves that if we pay more, we will get more. If your real reason for going to a particular school is going to Division I sports games in a huge stadium—just be honest with yourself. There are strategic reasons for overpaying for education, but many students' reasons have more to do with what they want to experience at college rather than the results they achieve *from* their college education. It's only four years later when the experience is used up and the bills come due that many young people realize their high-minded reasons were wishful thinking. If you're going to pay more than you need to, bounce your reasons off of someone who will be candid with you about whether or not you are lying to yourself. Wishful thinking is a sneaky, sneaky mental critter that causes overpaying.

One last thing on debt: being smart about investment debt does not mean you have to go after the highest paying or the "most practical" professions. Both Syler and I became pastors, a profession that usually requires an expensive education and pays a relatively small salary. Generating income isn't the *only* consideration, but it is a *necessary* one. The goal is to prepare yourself for work you can actually get, work that makes a contribution to others and society, and that pays your bills.

Debt isn't the only financial concern you need to be aware of. There are at least three other common financial mistakes to consider.

1. Taking too much student aid

You will probably spend money available to you. You can probably get more student aid than you need. Therefore, it is easy to spend student aid you don't need to, and rack up a considerable amount of unnecessary debt. And interest rates don't help. When they are high, you pay a lot in interest. When they are low, spending more is easy to rationalize. Statistically, most students do.

One way to motivate yourself not to spend more than you need is to calculate the loan repayment. For example, $45,000 at 3.5 percent interest, paid back over 10 years is 119 payments of $445. Just imagine writing that check every month until you're 32.

There are lots of places to cut costs. Many students buy too many meals on their meal plan. I moved from meal plans to cooking my own food over the course of four years. It both saved money and prepared me for when there would be no dining hall.

Buying used textbooks online can basically eliminate book expenses. If you buy a used book on a site like Amazon, you can sell the book for almost exactly what you paid for it. Shopping around for housing and sharing a room is also a good way to save money. Look out for coupon books and free perks that don't require you to sign up for something. Most college towns give away a lot of coupons for good deals. Pay attention at the grocery store, and learn to shop wisely now. Lastly, although on-campus jobs can be fun and convenient, settling for minimum wage pay is not the best use of your time. Look for something better—it will pay more and look better on your résumé.

2. Misusing a credit card

My friend Rick has an IQ of 150 and college credit card debt of $12,000. He admits he wasn't paying attention. Those people giving out free stuff in exchange for a credit card aren't your friends, and they're good at what they do. The average college student is carrying credit card debt of $3,175, up from $2,169 in 2004.

Building your credit is important, but racking up consumer debt is an extremely expensive way to build credit, and is more likely to destroy your credit than build it in the long run. Credit cards are the most convenient way of acquiring debt, and therefore the most effective mechanism to saddle you with debt and undermine the development of spending self-discipline. The habits of lavishness or frugality that you develop in these years will follow you for decades.

If you choose to carry a credit card, don't have more than one, have your parents' blessing, and never carry a balance greater than what you have in the bank. Remember, anything you buy with a credit card, you can also buy with a debit card. Yet with a debit card you avoid many of the pitfalls and hassles of credit card use.

3. Not budgeting and building financial discipline

Over these next four years, you will be setting fifty-year character trajectories. Spending wisely, living within your means, and building wealth do not happen naturally. They require both intentional thought and cultivated discipline.

Therefore, living by a budget is an absolutely necessary practice for financial success. Budgeting may seem tedious and boring, but if you don't know how much money you have or are spending, you will usually spend more than you wanted to.

It teaches you to turn off your "Wanter" because it forces you to see that buying one thing means going without another. Asking yourself the question, "Should I go out for dinner tonight?" is different from the realization, "If I go out for dinner tonight, then I can't go out with my friends on Friday."

The practice of budgeting will force you to keep track of expenditures in real time and to face the ratio of money you save or give versus the money you spend on entertainment.

Budget basics

Budgeting is simply making sure your expenses don't exceed your income. Therefore you have to plan all necessary expenses up front: housing, food, tuition, transportation, cell phone, giving and saving for future major purchases and emergencies. Only after all these are planned will you know what is available for fun or other discretionary spending. The key is getting something in place and using it—you can always adjust it as time goes on.

It's important to budget giving and savings from the very beginning. The first step in savings should be an emergency fund of about $1000, and then go from there. If you don't give and save *first* each month, you will find you won't do either.

It's especially important to start the spiritual discipline of giving when you're young and poor, so that when you're older and have more money, it will already be a normal part of your life. You may have heard this before, but unless you are committed to giving a portion of your money away, you will not own your possessions: they will own you. And there are always excuses to *not* give. Some claim they're too poor to possibly give anything. Others with more sizeable wealth believe they have too many expenses to give substantially. The Old Testament Scriptures are filled with references to giving out of your "firstfruits." That is, God wants you to be generous with what comes in on the front end of your income, and not out of what may or may not be left over once you've taken care of all of your expenses.

Entertainment and food expenses have to be budgeted for and tracked in real time or they will get away from you in a hurry. For many people having that money in cash in their wallet is the best way to make sure they can't overspend.

Practically, you may find you need to have fun and make meals with other people on budgets. It's hard to stay on a budget when you're spending money on food and entertainment with people who aren't. Therefore choosing your company will always affect your finances—they will either be helping you stay frugal or undermining the development of your financial self-discipline. We are either formed or deformed in community, so choose your companions wisely.

Final thought: Everyone needs a financial education

Your college education will not teach you everything you need to know. You need a spiritual education in following Jesus and understanding Scripture. You need a relational education about friendship and family. You also need a financial education. All three of these educations are incredibly painful to learn the hard way. You have to go out and get the education you need, because you don't want every lesson to come with a consequence. Concerning money, I think every young adult should take a major financial planning course. I like the Dave Ramsey course called Financial Peace University. There are a number of them, and taking one and applying it will be one of the best investments you could ever make in your life, and financial freedom makes the right relational and spiritual choices all the easier to make.

16.

WHAT YOU SHOULD KNOW ABOUT MARRIAGE

"That bwessed awangement. That dweam wiffin a dweam. Mawage. Have you the wing?"

If you never saw *The Princess Bride,* watch it as soon as you can. It's one of my all-time favorites. And one of the great things about it is the love story. The unlikely story of a servant boy who falls in love with his beautiful mistress, is taken away, believed to be dead, and then reunited with his love. They fight, defeat their enemies just in the nick of time, and ride off into the sunset, basking in the glow of their "true love." But where was *Princess Bride Part Two: The Marriage Years*? We never heard how ol' Wesley and Buttercup turned out. We just take for granted that they were happy. Why? Because it's just a fairy-tale.

Not too long ago, my family and I were reading stories before bedtime. I was finishing up the book version of Disney's Cinderella when I got to the last line: and they lived happily ever after. And I couldn't stop myself. I added, "Yeah, right." Heidi's eyes got huge: "Syler!" "Sorry," I clarified. "Just kidding, they really are happy, never have any problems, have never fought, even once; all smiles and butterflies every day!" Can you tell that even after more than fifteen years of being married to a woman that I love more than anyone in the world, I'm still a bit cynical when it comes to storybook endings?

When I was in college, I was in the musical *Into the Woods.* The show featured the mixing up of several fairy tales: Cinderella, Jack and the Beanstalk, Little Red Riding Hood, and others. The first act tells their story and weaves them all together. But just after they've wrapped up all of the plot lines, the narrator says: "To be continued!" And the second act could be subtitled "After the Ever After."

Times are tough again for everyone, frustrations are high, and the show ends with things like adultery and accidental deaths. Do those sound familiar to any of you? They should, because the second act takes it out of the realm of the fairy-tale and dares to wonder what happens to these people who seem so fulfilled in all of the storybooks.

Marriage is very hard work. There's a reason why half of all marriages end in divorce. Everyone who stands at the altar and looks into their spouse-to-be's eyes has every intention of fulfilling the vows that they share in front of God and everyone they know. But somewhere along the way things get hard, and around half the time the couple that deeply desired to be committed to each other for a lifetime ends up in court, citing irreconcilable differences or some other reason as the impetus for their split. Sadly, the divorce rate among Christians is reportedly just as high as for the rest of the world.

So what is it? Why do some marriages make it and some don't? I don't presume to know the full answer, but I do believe that some marriages fail because the couple has false expectations and misunderstandings about what marriage is about.

In light of that, then, I present to you what every college student needs to know about marriage. Some of you might be saying: oh great, Syler, marriage advice. How timely and practical. Why don't you give us some pointers on how to find the right nursing home while you're at it? Since *we're still teenagers, and none of us are married*!

I hear you, but the reality is that getting married is a priority for many of you even now, and it will be a popular topic of conversation during your college years. And besides, you never know just how soon you may need this advice. Nic and I were both married in our early twenties, and you could be too (don't worry—it's a good thing!).

It's important to have a realistic idea of marriage now, so that if it comes, you'll be prepared.

Not the goal of life

I want to start by making clear that getting married should never be anyone's life goal. The common joke on Christian campuses is that many female students are there to get their MRS degree (ring by spring!). This is backwards. Your goal upon entering college, and in all of life for that matter, should be to seek God and His Kingdom in all you do. Matthew 5 says that when we do that, everything else we need will be given to us as well. If He brings us a spouse along the way, then we'll continue seeking Him first as a married person. The reality is that getting married doesn't make you happy, and it doesn't eliminate your problems. You just exchange a single person's problems for a married person's problems.

Millions of unmarried Christians, both now and throughout church history, have had utterly complete and fulfilled lives without a spouse. In fact, Paul states his case in 1 Corinthians 7 that remaining unmarried is preferable to being married because a single person has undivided interests. Even though many of you might consider it a gift that you'd rather return, singleness is called a gift in the New Testament.

You cannot make marriage your goal; God must be your goal. Look at the example of Adam. God was his primary companion first, and at the right time, He brought along the spouse Adam needed. We can do the same.

Having said that, in Genesis God Himself says that it's not good for a man to be alone, and a great many of you at some point in your lives will walk down that aisle. There is nothing unholy about this, and it is not wrong for you to want to be married! Proverbs says that

"He who finds a wife finds what is good and receives favor from the Lᴏʀᴅ" (18:22). If God has given you the desire to be married, it is not a sinful desire. And it may or may not be one that He grants. In the meantime you can make Him your hope, while trusting in Him to provide the right person at the right time.

And the winner is . . .

But how do we know when the right time is, and who the perfect person will be? And is there only one "right person" for us? You can read my previous chapter to hear my view on finding the will of God, but suffice it to say that God will largely use your own heart's desire to lead you in this.

In terms of when, I would say you're ready to be married when you're ready to "leave and cleave" as Genesis 2 talks about. That is, you must feel like you're independent enough to separate yourself from your parents, you're financially capable of supporting yourself, and you have a strong desire to be united to your spouse both physically and emotionally. If that is coupled with the blessing of an authority figure in your life such as your pastor and the wise counsel of trusted friends, I'd say you are ready to get hitched.

As for whether there's one "right person," my answer is yes and no. I do believe that there are times when God sends the right person along, and it is clear that God has given you to each other. But if one of you decides to be disobedient and walks away, or marries some-one else, I don't believe that it means that the other person must be single forever. God may send another "right person" along. This is clear in the case of someone whose spouse dies. In such an instance, there are two "right people."

Two more pieces of advice are important. The Bible never instructs you to marry the person you love, but it does tell you to love the person you marry. That is, there are very limited instructions on choosing (we'll get to those), but lots of instructions on how to act once you've chosen.

The other bit of wisdom is that the prayer to pray is not: "send me the right spouse" but rather "make me the right spouse." Before you even worry about who your future spouse will be, ask God to make you into the kind of person that can selflessly love another. More on this in a minute. But first, some advice on how to view marriage.

Don't idealize it

I would estimate that around 90 percent of married life centers around the mundane activities of life. Let me give you a little quiz. Between writing the last sentence and this one, I got up from my desk and did the following:

a) I went to my notebook and wrote a love poem to my wife, in French.

b) I drove to the florist, and bought three red roses, one to represent me, one to represent Heidi, and one to represent our love.

c) Heidi and I had a four-hour candlelight dinner in which we stared into one another's eyes and renewed our wedding vows.

d) I folded laundry that was necessitated by one of my children's chronic diarrhea.

I think you know what the answer is. Especially when you add kids to the mix, life gets very full and your relationship with your spouse gets even more complicated than it already was. When you're dating, you have just two roles in your relationship: friend and lover, *philo* love and *eros* love. The world is wonderful and exciting, and your relationship is primarily selfish. Sure, you'll wrestle a bear to prove your love, but it's all still about you, not the other, because they make you feel so good all the time. But once you get married, you add at least the following roles: roommate, financial partner, and spiritual leader/follower. And then when kids come along, you now become co-CEOs of a joint business venture, which is figuring out how to raise the darn things you just made.

This is why marrying your best friend is an absolute must. This is the person you will be spending much of your time with. She's the person you will make countless decisions with. He's the person you will eat thousands of meals with.

Your spouse is the person that you get to "do life" with. And after the initial excitement of finally getting to be one with this person you love wears off, you're left primarily with a best friend and roommate. Now, your love only grows deeper, and I can honestly say that I love, respect, cherish, and admire Heidi more each year that I'm married to her. But it takes work. Getting married was easy, but staying married is one of the hardest things I've ever done. Marriage will bring out the best in you, but at times it will also bring out the absolute worst.

Before we were married, Heidi considered herself a pretty selfless person, and I would have agreed with her. This is one of the things that attracted me to her: her heart to serve and sacrifice for others. But being married has made her realize that she is actually an extremely selfish person, much to her frustration. What about me, you ask? Oh, I *knew* I was extremely selfish, so it wasn't a surprise. I would say that selfishness and pride are the two primary reasons marriages don't last. When you're first together, you'll do anything to lay down your own personal rights and desires for your significant other, but as time wears on, selfishness starts to creep in. "Why does *she* always get what she wants? I can't keep deferring to her all the time," he thinks. "All he thinks about is himself. It's time I got what *I* want," she thinks. And slowly, walls grow between them. If selfishness begins to build the wall, pride comes right on its heels and finishes the job. Pride is what keeps one of the two from finally saying: "I'm sorry. I'm being selfish. I love you and want what's best for you, even if it means I don't always get what I want." If you can learn how to swallow pride, deny your selfishness, and be willing to both offer and receive forgiveness, your marriage will be in great shape.

Make a good choice

Who you marry is, without a doubt, one of the biggest decisions you will make. So here, briefly, is some biblical advice along those lines, first for men: "Better to live on a corner of the roof than share a house with a quarrelsome wife" (Prov. 21:9). "A quarrelsome wife is like a constant dripping" (Prov. 19:13). "Charm is deceptive and beauty is fleeting, but a woman who fears the LORD is to be praised" (Prov. 31:30).

Guys, a "hot" wife simply will not cut it. If she's given to quarreling, you are in for a long marriage, like the drip . . . drip . . . drip of a leaky faucet. The final quote from Proverbs 31 could not be truer. How many of you have had a crush on someone only to discover later that you were just being deceived by her charm? And beauty is certainly fleeting, even in the days of plastic surgery. Most of you won't look any better than you do right now.

But if your wife fears God, if she has put her total hope in Him and in nothing else, then this will not fade; it will grow. And you will find that your love and admiration for her will grow as well.

And now for the ladies: "If a man is lazy, the rafters sag; if his hands are idle, the house leaks" (Eccles. 10:18). "Husbands, love your wives, just as Christ loved the church and gave himself up for her" (Eph. 5:25). First, what is the character of the man? Is he lazy, or hardworking? You, too, will have to live with the sound of a constant dripping, except yours will be the actual dripping of water from your leaky roof. And then, very importantly: is he willing to give up his life for you, as Christ did for the church? Does he show you that he's willing to serve and honor you?

Many of these things cannot be learned. Most people in a marriage have had to come to terms with the fact that they cannot change their spouse. That's why you say the words "for better or for worse" when you get married. Beyond these biblical guidelines, as I said before, marrying your best friend is ideal. Ask yourself: is this the person I'd rather be with than anyone else? If so, that's a good indicator.

Let your passions guide you

In 1970, the average age of first-time brides was 21, grooms 23. By 1998, the average age for women was up to 25, while for men it was 27. People in our country are waiting longer and longer to get married. In Christian circles, though, the age is often much lower. There's a very simple reason for this: Christians know that unless they're married, they can't have sex! I'll never forget the advice one of my mentors and dear friends gave to me when I started dating Heidi my senior year in college: let your sexual passion lead you to the altar. In other words, you have three options when it comes to what to do with your sexual passion. It can lead you to act on those passions, to marriage, or to break off the relationship because it's not the right choice.

Granted, there have been a number of Christian couples that have gotten married too young because they simply wanted to hop in the sack together. True, you should not enter into the decision lightly. But I believe that one of the purposes of our sex drive is to encourage us to not just act on our sexual desires when they strike our fancy. It is there to urge us to seek the appropriate way to act on them, inside the context of marriage. This will be much easier if you let the sleeping dog lie, and follow the advice in Song of Songs: "Do not arouse or awaken love until it so desires" (2:7). Your marriage day is the day to awaken love, and not before.

Once I'm there, how do I stay there?

John and Noël Piper picked a very curious passage to be read on their wedding day. It is from Habakkuk 3:17–18:

> Though the fig tree does not bud
>
> and there are no grapes on the vines,
>
> though the olive crop fails
>
> and the fields produce no food,
>
> though there are no sheep in the pen
>
> and no cattle in the stalls,
>
> yet I will rejoice in the LORD,
>
> I will be joyful in God my Savior.

You might think: those Pipers, so romantic. But they knew something that a lot of young couples don't know: staying married is hard work, and there will be times when you have nothing left. In fact, at times you will not want to love your spouse and you may even think about ending the marriage. The Pipers' point in choosing this passage was to communicate their intentions in spite of the worst possible scenarios. Even if everything around me is failing, I will continue to rejoice in God, and in so doing, I will continue to be faithful to the spouse He has brought me. You must be aware of the reality of this.

A study I heard about suggests that the average human falls in love six times in their life, three before they're married and three after they're married. You will often not be able to stop yourself from growing attracted to other people. I wish I could say that my awareness of other women stopped after I met Heidi. But that's not the way life works. What it means is that, *at all costs, forsaking ALL others,* you are faithful to your spouse. Period. Even if your sheep pen and cattle stalls are empty, and so is your heart, you remain faithful. And God will reward you in this.

May ours be the generation that turns the tide on marriage, that those of us to whom God grants a spouse would be faithful men and women. And regardless, we know that we *will* live happily ever after, not because of a spouse, but because of our God who loves us and redeemed us and will prepare a place for us with Him in eternity.

YOUR STORY

You've read our stories. And you've read the stories of some of our friends and former students, who have shared their triumphs and their regrets. It's now time for you to write your own story during your time in college. There's no one else who can write it, just you.

We'd love to hear more about your story, and for you to be encouraged by others who are using *Game Plan* to encourage them to embrace this path of wisdom.

Go to www.gameplan4college.com to join the *Game Plan* network of students. You'll find an extended bibliography, tips for turning this book into a retreat for graduating seniors, and additional testimonies.

ABOUT THE AUTHORS

Nic Gibson (MDiv, Trinity International University) spent more than a decade in student, camping, and college ministry. He is now lead pastor of High Point Church, Madison, Wisconsin, a city that is home to more than 30,000 university students. He's spoken to youth and college groups in New York, Illinois, Florida, California, Wisconsin, and India, and continues to work with students dealing with tough questions and making big choices. He lives in Madison with his wife, Alexi, two daughters, and one son.

Syler Thomas (MDiv, Trinity Evangelical Divinity School) is a native Texan who has been the High School Pastor at Christ Church Lake Forest in Illinois since 1998. He writes a column for *Youthworker Journal*, has had articles published in *Leadership Journal* and the *Chicago Tribune*, and is the coauthor of *The Jesus Creed for Students* with Scot McKnight and Chris Folmsbee. He and his wife, Heidi, have four kids.

ABOUT PARACLETE PRESS

Who We Are

Paraclete Press is a publisher of books, recordings, and DVDs on Christian spirituality. Our publishing represents a full expression of Christian belief and practice—from Catholic to Evangelical, from Protestant to Orthodox.

We are the publishing arm of the Community of Jesus, an ecumenical monastic community in the Benedictine tradition. As such, we are uniquely positioned in the marketplace without connection to a large corporation and with informal relationships to many branches and denominations of faith.

What We Are Doing

Paraclete Press Books Paraclete publishes books that show the richness and depth of what it means to be Christian. Although Benedictine spirituality is at the heart of all that we do, we publish books that reflect the Christian experience across many cultures, time periods, and houses of worship. We publish books that nourish the vibrant life of the church and its people.

We have several different series, including the best-selling Paraclete Essentials and Paraclete Giants series of classic texts in contemporary English; Voices from the Monastery—men and women monastics writing about living a spiritual life today; award-winning poetry; best-selling gift books for children on the occasions of baptism and first communion; and the Active Prayer Series that brings creativity and liveliness to any life of prayer.

Mount Tabor Books Paraclete's newest series, Mount Tabor Books, focuses on liturgical worship, art and art history, ecumenism, and the first millennium church, and was created in conjunction with the Mount Tabor Ecumenical Centre for Art and Spirituality in Barga, Italy.

Paraclete Recordings From Gregorian chant to contemporary American choral works, our recordings celebrate the best of sacred choral music composed through the centuries that create a space for heaven and earth to intersect. Paraclete Recordings is the record label representing the internationally acclaimed choir Gloriæ Dei Cantores, praised for their "rapt and fathomless spiritual intensity" by *American Record Guide*; the Gloriæ Dei Cantores Schola, specializing in the study and performance of Gregorian chant; and the other instrumental artists of the Gloriæ Dei Artes Foundation.

Paraclete Press is also privileged to be the exclusive North American distributor of the recordings of the Monastic Choir of St. Peter's Abbey in Solesmes, France, long considered to be a leading authority on Gregorian chant.

Paraclete Video Our DVDs offer spiritual help, healing, and biblical guidance for a broad range of life issues including grief and loss, marriage, forgiveness, facing death, bullying, addictions, Alzheimer's, and spiritual formation.

Learn more about us at our website:
www.paracletepress.com, or call us toll-free at 1-800-451-5006.

SCAN
TO
READ
MORE

DO YOU KNOW THE JESUS CREED?

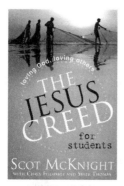

ISBN: 978-1-55725-883-0
$13.99 Trade paperback

The Jesus Creed for Students

Essential Christian formation for anyone
between the ages of 16 and 22.

The gravity point of a life before God is that his
followers are to love God and love others with
everything they have. Scot McKnight calls this
the Jesus Creed. Now, he's worked it out with
high school and college students, seeking to
show how this double commandment to love
makes sense and gives shape to the moral lives
of young adults. *The Jesus Creed for Students* aims
to demonstrate a simple truth—that followers
of Jesus really follow Jesus. (Also, it's practical,
filled with stories, and backed up and checked by
youth pastors.)

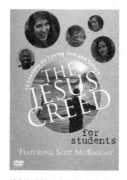

ISBN: 978-1-61261-075-7
$29.95 54 min. DVD

The Jesus Creed for Students
The DVD
Twelve Lessons on Loving God and Loving Others

The perfect tool for groups, this DVD provides
an engaging twelve-week study on the key
aspects of becoming a Jesus follower.